RISING★STARS

More Problem Solving and Reasoning

Open-ended activities to develop children's problem solving and reasoning skills

YEAR 4

ISBN: 978 1 51040 366 6

First published in 2017 by

Rising Stars UK Ltd, part of Hodder Education Group
An Hachette UK Company
Carmelite House
50 Victoria Embankment
London EC4Y 0DZ

www.risingstars-uk.com

Authors: Tim Handley, Paul Wrangles, Nicki Allman

Publisher: Alexandra Riley

Project Manager: Estelle Lloyd

Editorial: Jan Fisher, Denise Moulton

Cover design: Words & Pictures Ltd

Design: Steve Evans

Typesetting: Aptara

Illustrations: Aptara

Printed by Ashford Colour Press Ltd, Gosport, Hants

A catalogue record for this title is available from the British Library.

Acknowledgements

The authors and publisher would like to thank the staff and pupils at the following schools who trialled the *More Problem Solving and Reasoning* resources and provided material for the Case Study conversation snippets across the series:

Bentley CEVC Primary School, Bentley, Ipswich
Bignold Primary School and Nursery, Norwich
Copdock Primary School, Copdock, Suffolk
Cutnall Green First School, Cutnall Green, Worcs
Delce Junior School, Rochester, Kent
Ditchingham Primary School, Ditchingham, Suffolk
Donington Cowley Endowed Primary School, Donington, Lincs
Eccleston CE Primary School, Chester, Cheshire
Garden Suburb Junior School, London
Gillingham St Michael's Primary School, Gillingham, Beccles, Suffolk
Hapton CEVC Primary School, Hapton, Norwich
Harleston CEVA Primary School, Harleston, Norfolk
Piddle Valley CEVA First School, Piddletrenthide, Dorchester, Dorset
St Barnabas CE Primary, Warrington
St Francis de Sales Catholic Junior School, Walton, Liverpool
St Martha's Catholic Primary School, Kings Lynn, Norfolk
St Nicholas CE Primary, Hurst, Reading, Berkshire
Well Lane Primary School, Birkenhead, Wirral
Woodlands Primary Academy, Great Yarmouth, Norfolk
Worfield Endowed CE Primary School, Worfield, Bridgnorth, Shropshire

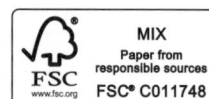

MIX
Paper from
responsible sources
FSC
www.fsc.org   FSC® C011748

Contents

Introduction

Rising Stars Maths *More Problem Solving and Reasoning*

This resource is designed to help teachers develop a 'reasoning classroom' where problem solving and reasoning form an integral part of each maths lesson. It provides key strategies to help teachers achieve this, together with extended investigation activities.

The book for each year group can be used in a variety of ways:

- individually
- in conjunction with the first *Problem Solving and Reasoning* book
- alongside any other scheme, planning framework or maths resource.

Problem solving and reasoning in the 2014 National Curriculum and national tests

The aims of the 2014 National Curriculum for Mathematics place a significant emphasis on the development of children's problem-solving and reasoning skills. It is the government's expectation that all the content of the curriculum is taught through these aims.

Below are the aims of the curriculum, with the key elements relating to problem solving and reasoning underlined.

'The National Curriculum for Mathematics aims to ensure that all pupils:

- become **fluent** in the fundamentals of mathematics, including through varied and frequent practice with <u>increasingly complex problems over time</u>, so that pupils develop conceptual understanding and the ability to recall and <u>apply knowledge</u> rapidly and accurately

- <u>**reason mathematically** by following a line of enquiry, conjecturing relationships and generalisations, and developing an argument, justification or proof using mathematical language</u>

- <u>can **solve problem**s by applying their mathematics to a variety of routine and non-routine problems with increasing sophistication, including breaking down problems into a series of simpler steps and persevering in seeking solutions.</u>

Mathematics is an interconnected subject in which pupils need to be able to move <u>fluently between representations of mathematical ideas</u>. The Programmes of Study are, by necessity, organised into apparently distinct domains, but pupils should make <u>rich connections across mathematical ideas</u> to develop fluency, <u>mathematical reasoning</u> and competence in <u>solving increasingly sophisticated problems</u>.'

These aims extend problem solving and reasoning beyond simple worded problems.

Within the Programmes of Study, very few statements specifically related to problem solving and reasoning are provided. To help teachers develop a range of problem-solving skills, suggested objectives have been developed and are provided on pages 14 and 15.

In addition, the structure and content of the Key Stage 1 and Key Stage 2 National Curriculum tests (SATs) now reflect these aims, with a significant emphasis on children's ability to solve problems and reason.

It is only through constant exposure, practice and development of these core skills that children will be able to succeed both against the National Curriculum and in the statutory assessments. For this reason it is important that, when planning maths lessons, teachers always keep the aims of the curriculum in mind and incorporate problem-solving and reasoning opportunities into every lesson.

About the authors

Tim Handley

Tim Handley is a school leader, maths consultant and trainer working in East Anglia who has been involved in the authorship of 23 different published resources for schools. He is a Mathematics Specialist Teacher and accredited NCETM Professional Development Lead (Primary). He has a deep-seated passion for ensuring all children develop a true conceptual understanding of mathematics.

Paul Wrangles

Paul Wrangles taught at Key Stage 2 for nine years. He started Sparky Teaching (www.sparkyteaching.com) with his wife, with the aim of providing creative resources for teachers. He is an experienced author of educational resources, including resources for NCETM, Rising Stars, Hodder, Harper Collins and Discovery Education. All his writing reflects his particular interest in investigative and real-life maths.

Nicki Allman

Nicki Allman is a former senior leader in primary, a mathematics lead and a Mathematics Specialist Teacher, in the UK and abroad. She is now a writer of educational resources and activities. She is a passionate advocate of ensuring that children develop a deep conceptual understanding of mathematics, which can be developed through the use of problem solving and reasoning.

How to use the resources

Structure

This resource is split into two sections:

• *Key strategies*
• *Activities and investigations*

At the back of the book you will also find a glossary of useful mathematical terms. All the supporting resources, including editable PowerPoint prompt posters and Word files of the resource sheets, can be found on My Rising Stars.

Key strategies

This section provides 16 constructs or routines which can be used to integrate problem solving and reasoning into every maths lesson. Each key strategy is accompanied by a full explanation, tips for its use and a number of different examples of how the strategy could be used in different areas of mathematics to develop reasoning.

The examples provided are drawn from many areas of the mathematics curriculum. They are intended as starting points, which can then be taken and developed for use in all areas of mathematics. Through a careful and structured approach, teachers should embed these key strategies into their day-to-day teaching.

Each strategy also contains a conversation snippet from a case study from the schools where these resources have been trialled.

Note that the content of some examples is pitched slightly below the equivalent year content objectives in the Programmes of Study. This is to allow children to focus on the development of their reasoning skills, using subject knowledge with which they are already familiar.

On My Rising Stars there are CPD videos showing the key strategies in action in the classroom to further support teachers as they introduce and embed the approaches.

Activities and investigations

This section provides 18 extended problem-solving activities. These all develop one or more key problem-solving and reasoning skills, as well as covering an area of the 2014 National Curriculum for Mathematics. In every year group, the final four activities and investigations are set in the context of space. This makes it possible to run a maths week across the whole school using problems that have the same context.

Each activity will last a minimum of one hour and can, in many cases, be developed further. The resources for each activity comprise:

• Detailed teacher guidance which includes a learning objective, curriculum links, background knowledge and a step-by-step teaching sequence. The guidance also provides key questions to help develop reasoning (which use one or more of the key strategies). Ideas about how to adapt the activity for those who require further support and how the activity could be extended to meet the needs of more able mathematicians are also included.

• A prompt poster to display on the interactive whiteboard to introduce the problem to the children. This includes the background to the problem, the main challenge or challenges, plus 'Things to think about' prompts to help develop children's reasoning skills. Full colour versions of the posters can be found on My Rising Stars as editable PowerPoint files. They are also reproduced in 'The problem' section of the teacher guidance for ease of reference. Some of the PowerPoint presentations include additional prompt poster slides that can be used to aid differentiation, by providing easier and harder versions of the problem, or to scaffold the teaching by introducing the challenge one step at a time.

Maths superpowers CPD

John Mason[1] has identified a set of eight 'mathematical powers' that all children possess and which we need to foster and develop in order to create 'able mathematicians' who can reason about maths and solve problems. The powers, which come in pairs, are as follows:

Conjecture

Children should be encouraged to **make conjectures**, that is, say what they think about what they notice or why something happens. For example, a conjecture made by a child could be, 'I think that when you multiply an odd number by an even number, you are always going to end up with an even number'.

and

Convince

Children should then be encouraged to **convince**, that is, to persuade people (a partner, group, class, teacher, an adult at home, etc.) that their conjectures are true. In the process of convincing, children may use some, or all, of their other 'maths powers'.

Organise

Children should be encouraged to **organise**, putting things (numbers, facts, patterns, shapes, etc.) into groups, an order or a pattern.

and

Classify

Children should then be encouraged to **classify** the objects they have organised, e.g. identifying the groups as odd and even numbers, irregular and regular shapes, etc.

Imagine

Children should be encouraged to **imagine** objects, patterns, numbers and resources to help them solve problems and reason about mathematics.

and

Express

Children should be encouraged to **express their thinking**, that is, to show and explain their thinking and reasoning, e.g. about a problem, relationship or generalisation.

Specialise

Children should be encouraged to **specialise**, that is, to look at specific examples or a small set of examples of something. For example, looking at the odd number 7 and the even number 8 to test their conjecture that odd × even number = even number. Children can also specialise in order to start to see patterns and relationships and make generalisations.

and

Generalise

Children should be encouraged to **generalise**, that is, to make connections and use these to form rules and patterns. For example, from their specific example they could generalise that any odd number multiplied by any even number gives an even number. Children should also be encouraged to use algebra to express their generalisations.

These 'maths superpowers' have become the central foundation of many maths teacher development programmes, including the Mathematics Specialist Teacher (MaST) programme. The key strategies and investigations in this resource have been developed to foster these superpowers.

[1] Mason, J. and Johnston-Wilder, S. (eds) (2004) Learners' Powers in: *Fundamental Constructs in Mathematics Education*, London: RoutledgeFalmer, pp.115–142

Developing reasoning CPD

Reasoning and conceptual understanding

Encouraging children to reason in maths helps to support children to develop a conceptual and relational understanding of maths: an understanding of *why* maths 'works', rather than just following a set of instructions. This leads to a far greater understanding and confidence in maths.

Developing a reasoning classroom

1   Begin by choosing a few of the key strategies provided in the first section of this resource and introducing them to your class. Many of these strategies, such as 'Always, sometimes, never', 'Strange and obvious' and 'What's the same, what's different?' can also be extended to form whole lessons in their own right, which may be useful when children first experience the strategy.

2   Allow the strategies to form part of your day-to-day questioning so that children become familiar with using them. If these routines are used regularly, children will quickly get used to structuring their thoughts in this way.

3   Use the extended problems in the *Activities and investigations* section. These provide opportunities for children to develop their reasoning skills over a prolonged activity. Each activity includes suggestions of how the key strategies could be incorporated to develop children's thinking as they work on the investigations.

Cross-curricular reasoning

Of course, children's natural ability to reason extends beyond mathematics. The key strategies and approaches explained in this resource can easily be used across the curriculum. For example, in a geography-based lesson children could be asked: *What's the same, what's different about these two settlements*? Alternatively, in an English lesson, children could be asked to identify the 'odd one out' in a selection of words.

Embedding problem solving and reasoning throughout the school

A structured approach to introducing the key strategies and approaches will help to embed problem solving and reasoning across your school. It is important that reasoning and problem solving become part of every maths lesson, rather than a 'one day a week' occurrence.

It is suggested that schools and teachers introduce the key strategies gradually, allowing both children and teachers to become familiar with them and teachers to begin to incorporate them into their day-to-day teaching. A suggested 30-week sequence for introducing all the key strategies is provided on My Rising Stars.

Problem-solving techniques   CPD

This section offers a number of suggestions that are useful to consider when organising and supporting children to encourage reasoning in the classroom.

USE ME

When supporting children in problem-solving and reasoning activities, the stages below, which form the 'USE ME' mnemonic, are useful to follow.

- **Understanding:** Check that children understand the problem, activity or statement that has been given. Does it need rewording or further explanation? Do they have the subject knowledge needed?

- **Specialising:** Start by asking children to specialise by looking at, or creating, one specific example. This then can be extended to looking at/creating a small group of examples. By specialising, children are more likely to be able to explore the structure of the mathematics, before widening out to make connections and generalisations.

- **Encouraging representations:** The use of representations is vital as they significantly enhance children's experience and understanding of mathematics. Representations can take many forms including practical apparatus (such as bead strings, counters, cubes, etc.), recording/jottings (such as number lines) and internal (internalised versions of representations that children visualise and imagine). Children should also be encouraged to create their own representations. Encourage children to think about how they could represent the statement, or how they could represent specific examples of the statement.

- **Making generalisations:** After children have looked at, and often represented, specialised examples, they can begin to explore the connections between their examples. Can they make a statement that applies to all examples? If no generalised statement is possible, can they make a statement that applies to some examples (and define which examples this applies to)? Can they explain why it is not possible to make a generalisation?

- **Extending:** Provide a further, linked, question or investigation for children to explore.

It is important to note that, in some contexts, not all stages of USE ME will be appropriate.

Grouping for problem solving and reasoning

Teachers often ask how it is best to group children for problem-solving and reasoning tasks. Variety is really the key here! Below are some forms of groups for you to consider:

- **Familiar maths partners** whom children work with frequently in maths and with whom they are able to communicate well.

- **Pairs of friends** who enjoy working together.

- **Challenge trios** (groups of three), which can provide a good basis for discussion and development of ideas.

- **Mixed-ability pairs or groups**, which have often been shown to raise attainment for all children in the group: the lower-attaining children benefit from the peer coaching from the higher-attaining children, whilst the higher-attaining children have to extend their understanding and thinking further in order to explain it clearly to others.

- **Same-ability pairs or groups** also, of course, have their place as they allow the task to be closely matched to children's ability.

It is important that children become used to working in different types of groups. In this way, they develop flexibility and become adept at explaining their thinking and reasoning to a wide range of people. Different tasks will, of course, suit different ways of grouping.

Panic envelopes to facilitate self-differentiation

These are a great strategy to enable self-differentiation of problem-solving and reasoning activities. Inside an envelope, place one or more items that will support children in carrying out the activity; then place the envelopes either in the middle of a group's table and/or on a maths working wall.

The content of the envelopes can be varied, and could include:

- additional information

- key questions to help develop thinking

- conjectures for children to prove/disprove

- specific examples

- partly or fully worked solutions to part of the problem.

Give children the challenge of taking part in the activity independently, but let them know that at any point during the activity they can self-select to open the panic envelope and read one or more of the items that you have placed inside. Adults in the classroom can also suggest to children that they may benefit from opening the panic envelope if they become stuck while working through an activity. The content of the envelopes can be further differentiated for different groups of children.

Envoy

This technique enables ideas to be shared between different groups. Having given children time to discuss their own thoughts, conjectures and generalisations in groups, each group then sends an 'envoy' to share their discussions with another group.

The envoy could be chosen by the group or selected by the teacher. By randomly selecting the envoy, you will help ensure that every child in the group understands the thinking, conjectures or generalisations of the group as any one of them may be called upon to explain them to another group.

As a further extension, the envoy can be asked to bring back a summary of the thoughts from the group they visited to their 'home' group, so that the groups can consider new ideas and revisit their own thinking in light of the other conjectures.

Graffiti maths

'Graffiti maths' is an approach to problem-solving and reasoning tasks which encourages children to think and work 'big'. It was developed almost simultaneously by a number of teachers, including Claire Lotriet[2] and Geoff Barton in 2012.

Graffiti maths involves children working together as a team on a problem or investigation, working on tables that are covered in 'magic whiteboard' sheets, large pieces of paper (taped down) or another covering which allows children to write 'on' the tables. Some teachers also choose to remove the chairs from the classroom, which encourages children to move around the table.

This approach encourages children to work together and gives them ample space to explore ideas, test conjectures and make connections. The recording space is shared, which means that one child is less likely to take 'ownership' of it whilst others hang back and 'lurk' in the background. The act of sharing the recording space also encourages maths talk and creates a generally 'buzzy' atmosphere in your classroom.

Children can also move around and look at different tables and their recording, which can be a very useful plenary or mid-session activity.

Think, pair, share

This strategy is particularly effective during shared learning. This is a development of simple paired talk. Ask a question (usually open-ended) and give children a period of thinking time (normally one to two minutes works best) for them to 'privately' think about the question or problem posed. Next, give children some time to discuss the question/thinking with a partner, before the partners share their thinking with another pair (so forming groups of four).

[2] http://clairelotriet.com/blog/2012/12/15/graffiti-maths/

Snowballing

After giving time for paired discussion, the discussion can then be 'snowballed'. Ask pairs to share with another pair and then ask these groups to snowball together and discuss with another group (forming groups of eight). Depending on class size, this can be repeated again (forming groups of 16) before each of the 'snowballed' groups feeds back to the whole class.

Maths journals

It can be beneficial to provide children with a book or space in addition to their normal maths book. If possible, the book should contain plain paper so that thinking is not constrained or formalised by squares or lines. This book can be used by children to explore their thinking, approaches and ideas, without the worry of it being seen or needing to meet your school's presentation standards. Maths journals should not be formally marked; a maths journal is the child's own space to explore ideas before transferring some of them to their main maths book or other format.

WWW and EBI as a plenary

A useful activity for the plenary session is to ask children **W**hat **W**ent **W**ell (WWW) in the activity and what would be **E**ven **B**etter **I**f (EBI). A ratio of four WWWs to one EBI is often effective, as this encourages children to focus on the positives and strengths from the session. The phrase 'even better if …' encourages children to be constructive in their suggestions for improvement. So, rather than saying 'We didn't work together very well', children might phrase an EBI as 'It would have been even better if we had listened more to what each other said so that we could share our thinking together'.

Assessing progress

Accurate assessment of children's problem-solving and reasoning skills is only possible through observation of and conversations with the child, together with evidence from their recorded work. The bank of evidence of a child's problem-solving and reasoning ability will naturally be built up over time, as children experience and take part in a range of different activities.

The objectives in the charts on the following pages can be used when planning and assessing the problem-solving and reasoning elements of the 2014 National Curriculum for Mathematics.

Problem-solving and reasoning objectives

Year 1	Year 2	Year 3
• Describe a puzzle or problem using numbers, practical materials and diagrams; use these to solve the problem and set the solution in the original context. • Order and arrange combinations of objects and shapes in patterns. • Answer a question by selecting and using suitable equipment, and sorting information, shapes or objects; display results using tables and pictures. • Describe simple patterns and relationships involving numbers or shapes; decide whether examples satisfy given conditions. • Describe ways of solving puzzles and problems, explaining choices and decisions orally or using pictures.	• Identify and record the information or calculation needed to solve a puzzle or problem; carry out the steps or calculations and check the solution in the context of the problem. • Follow a line of enquiry; answer questions by choosing and using suitable equipment and selecting, organising and presenting information in lists, tables and simple diagrams. • Describe patterns and relationships involving numbers or shapes; make predictions and test these with examples. • Present solutions to puzzles and problems in an organised way; explain decisions, methods and results in pictorial, spoken or written form, using mathematical language and number sentences.	• Represent the information in a puzzle or problem using numbers, images or diagrams; use these to find a solution and present it in context, where appropriate using £.p notation or units of measure. • Follow a line of enquiry by deciding what information is important; make and use lists, tables and graphs to organise and interpret the information. • Identify patterns and relationships involving numbers or shapes, and use these to solve problems. • Express the rules for sequences in words (e.g. 3, 5, 7: you add 2 each time). • Begin to make generalisations based on patterns in mathematics (e.g. all even numbers end in 0, 2, 4, 6 or 8). • Begin to make conjectures (statements) about mathematics and develop the ability to convince others (e.g. when continuing a pattern). • Begin to make 'if … then …' statements (e.g. if 2 + 4 = 6 then 6 − 2 = 4). • Describe and explain methods, choices and solutions to puzzles and problems orally and in writing, using pictures and diagrams.

Year 4	Year 5	Year 6
• Represent a puzzle or problem using number sentences, statements or diagrams; use these to solve the problem; present and interpret the solution in the context of the problem.	• Represent a puzzle or problem by identifying and recording the information or calculations needed to solve it; find possible solutions and confirm them in the context of the problem.	• Tabulate systematically the information in a problem or puzzle; identify and record the steps or calculations needed to solve it, using symbols where appropriate; interpret solutions in the original context and check their accuracy.
• Suggest a line of enquiry and the strategy needed to follow it; collect, organise and interpret selected information to find answers.	• Plan and pursue an enquiry; present evidence by collecting, organising and interpreting information; suggest extensions to the enquiry.	• Suggest, plan and develop lines of enquiry; collect, organise and represent information; interpret results and review methods; identify and answer related questions.
• Identify and use patterns, relationships and properties of numbers or shapes; investigate a statement involving numbers and test it with examples.	• Explore patterns, properties and relationships and propose a general statement involving numbers or shapes; identify examples for which the statement is true or false.	• Represent and interpret sequences, patterns and relationships involving numbers and shapes; suggest and test hypotheses; construct and use simple expressions and formulae in words and then symbols.
• Express the rules for increasingly complex sequences in words (e.g. 3, 6, 12, 24: you double each time).	• Explain reasoning using diagrams, graphs and text; refine ways of recording using images and symbols.	• Explain reasoning and conclusions, using words, symbols or diagrams as appropriate; use simple formulae expressed in words; express missing number problems algebraically (e.g. $6 + n = 28$).
• Report solutions to puzzles and problems, giving explanations and reasoning orally and in writing, using diagrams and symbols.	• Begin to express missing number problems algebraically (e.g. $7 + n = 12$).	• Begin to use symbols and letters to represent variables (things that can change) and unknowns in mathematics situations which they already understand, such as missing numbers, missing lengths, arithmetical rules (e.g. $a + b = b + a$) and number puzzles (e.g. two numbers total 6, therefore $a + b = 6$).
• Continue to make generalisations based on patterns in mathematics.	• Continue to make increasingly advanced generalisations based on patterns in mathematics.	• Continue to make increasingly advanced generalisations based on patterns in mathematics.
	• Make conjectures (statements) about mathematics and further develop the ability to convince others.	• Make conjectures (statements) about mathematics and further develop the ability to convince others.
	• Continue to make 'if … then …' statements.	• Continue to make 'if … then …' statements, representing them using letters if able (e.g. if $2 + 4 = 6$, then $6 - 2 = 4$; represented using letters: if $a + b = c$, then $c - a = b$).

Key strategy

Give the children a statement and then ask whether it is always, sometimes or never true.

Why it's effective

This line of questioning encourages children to think about the concept of mathematical proof and allows them to develop the key skill of proving or disproving a statement. This key strategy is very effective for encouraging children to make connections between different areas of mathematics and for encouraging generalisations and algebraic thinking.

Tips for use

This key strategy makes a particularly effective starter activity. It can also be effective when introducing a new focus or concept. It works particularly well if time is allowed for paired or grouped discussion, with children encouraged to discuss the statement together and come up with their answer (always, sometimes, never) and justification before feeding back to you or the class. You can play 'devil's advocate', giving children different examples to check against their decision. It can also work well to give children a statement about which they may have misconceptions.

The strategy can also be used as a powerful assessment tool by asking the same 'always, sometimes, never' question at the start and end of a topic. Through doing this you should be able to notice and evidence the increased sophistication in children's thinking and reasoning skills.

Children can be given sets of statements to sort into 'always true', 'sometimes true' or 'never true'. These statements could be from one area of mathematics (e.g. fractions) or a mixture of areas. The activity can also be extended to ask how the statements can be changed to make them always true, sometimes true or never true.

Children should be encouraged to move towards generalised statements and, if they are able, algebraic representations of their answer, especially when the statement is 'always true'.

Watch out

! **Children may ask what you need in order to say that something is always true.**

This can be used as a really effective discussion point about the nature of mathematical proof. Ask: *How many examples do you need to give to prove a statement is not true? What do you need to do to prove a statement is always true?*

! **Children may jump to 'never' or 'always' answers.**

This can be used as an effective way to get children to discuss and consider other possibilities, and the 'Another, another, another' key strategy can be used here. Sometimes providing a counter-example to children, and asking them to find other examples, can also be beneficial. Ask: *Can you think of another example? What about if you had … ? Can you find some more examples where it is true/never true?*

Try these

Here are some examples to introduce your class to this strategy. In these examples, the content level is sometimes lower than that set out in the National Curriculum for Year 4. This is to allow children to focus on the development of reasoning skills, without being restricted by subject knowledge.

Case studies from the classroom

A snippet from a conversation between two Year 4 children discussing this question: *Is it always, sometimes or never true that multiplication makes a number bigger?*

Is it always, sometimes or never true that multiples of 9 are also multiples of 3?
➤ *Can you list some multiples of 9 and 3?*
➤ *What do you notice?*
➤ *Why might this be the case?*
➤ *What other relationships like this can you find?*

Is it always, sometimes or never true that, when you find 1 000 more than a number, you just increase the thousands digit by 1?
➤ *Is there a case when this wouldn't happen?*
➤ *Why is this?*

Is it always, sometimes or never true that, when counting in multiples of 25 from 0, the ones digit will always be 5 or 0?
➤ *What pattern do you notice about multiples of 25?*
➤ *Are there any other sets of multiples which share the same pattern?*

Is it always, sometimes or never true that adding two 4-digit numbers will give you a 4-digit number?
➤ *Can you think of any examples when this doesn't happen?*
➤ *Are there any rules that could help us predict when this does happen?*

Is it always, sometimes or never true that you can use addition to check the answer to a subtraction question?
➤ *How could you do this?*
➤ *Does it work for any subtraction question?*

Is it always, sometimes or never true that every HTO × O multiplication has to be done using a written method?
➤ *Can you think of any HTO × O multiplication you could do mentally?*
➤ *Can you decide on some rules if you need to use a written method?*

Is it always, sometimes or never true that every fraction has an equivalent fraction?
➤ *What is an equivalent fraction?*
➤ *How can we find equivalent fractions?*

Is it always, sometimes or never true that you find the decimal equivalent of a fraction with a denominator of 10 by dividing by 10?
➤ *Can you draw a diagram to help you check this?*
➤ *Why doesn't the denominator change?*

Is it always, sometimes or never true that to find a fraction of a number you just divide the number by the denominator?
➤ *Does this work for any fraction?*
➤ *Can you change the statement so that it is always true?*

Is it always, sometimes or never true that when you divide a number by 10 you just remove the last digit?
➤ *When might this appear to be happening?*

Is it always, sometimes or never true that there are 365 days in a year?
➤ *Are there any years for which this isn't the case?*
➤ *When do these occur?*

🔍 Activities and investigations

1 The Queen's lawn mower
3 The curious postman
4 Making 28
13 Mixed-up offers
14 Mr Shah's swimming pool shambles

Child A: Well, all the ones I've tried so far do, so it must be always true.

Child B: Let's think more though. What about if you multiplied a decimal number?

2 Another, another, another

Key strategy

Give the children a statement and ask them to give you examples that meet the statement, and then ask for another example, and another …

Why it's effective

This strategy encourages children to give specific examples which meet a given general statement. By asking them to repeatedly give another example that meets the statement, children develop their skills of specialising, that is, the skill of giving specific examples. This strategy also provides a good opportunity to assess children's conceptual understanding of an area of mathematics.

Tips for use

Initially ask children for one example that meets the criteria set and then, after a pause, ask for another. Continue doing this, pausing slightly each time to allow children to think about and construct their response, until children have exhausted the possible responses and/or a generalisation has been made.

You can focus the use of this strategy by introducing caveats (e.g. *Give me another that involves a negative number.*).

This strategy can be used in conjunction with other key strategies in this book, including 'If this is the answer, what's the question?' and 'Strange and obvious'.

It is useful to analyse children's methods for creating their responses – do they have a structured approach to generating further responses, are they using generalisations, or do their answers appear to be given at random?

You should encourage children to make generalisations by focusing on what their responses have in common. After generating responses independently, children could be encouraged to discuss their responses and draw out what they have in common. They could also discuss and compare their responses with a partner or wider group.

The activity can be extended further by asking children how many possible answers there are, asking them to convince you that their response is true. This is especially interesting if there is an infinite number of responses, as the reason for this can be explored. Mathematical thinking can also be developed further by asking children to convince you of the lowest and highest possible answers.

Watch out

Children may stick to one rule/generalisation where there are other possible options.

Whilst the generating of generalisations can be a valuable outcome from using this strategy, sometimes this will not be the intended outcome and children will become 'fixed' on a certain rule or generalisation in order to generate each response. In these instances simply modifying the statement by introducing a caveat is an effective way to focus children's thinking.

Try these

Here are some examples to introduce your class to this strategy. In these examples, the content level is sometimes lower than that set out in the National Curriculum for Year 4. This is to allow children to focus on the development of reasoning skills, without being restricted by subject knowledge.

Case studies from the classroom

A snippet from a conversation between two Year 4 children discussing this question: *Can you give me a way of partitioning 2 108? Another, another, another.*

Can you give me an example of two numbers with a difference of 7? Another, another, another.
➤ *What if you had to include a number smaller than 1?*
➤ *What if you had to include a number greater than 100?*
➤ *What if both numbers had to be bigger than 1 000?*
➤ *What if you had to use fractions?*

Can you give me an example of a multiple of 7? Another, another, another.
➤ *What if it had to be an even number?*
➤ *What if it had to be over 70?*
➤ *What if it had to be over 140?*

Can you give me an example of a way of partitioning the number 4 567? Another, another, another.
➤ *What If you couldn't partition it into thousands, hundreds, tens and ones?*
➤ *What if one of your partitions had to be 167?*
➤ *What if one of your partitions had to be an odd number?*
➤ *What if you had to partition into more than four numbers?*
➤ *What if one of the numbers had to be greater than 4 550?*

Can you give me an example of a number less than 0.5? Another, another, another.
➤ *What if it had to be a whole number?*
➤ *What if it had to be greater than $\frac{1}{4}$?*
➤ *What if it had to be a fraction?*

Can you give me an example of a common multiple of 3 and 6? Another, another, another.
➤ *What if it had to be above 60?*
➤ *What if it couldn't end in 6?*
➤ *What if it had to end in 8?*

Can you give me an example of numbers that multiply together to make 24? Another, another, another.
➤ *What if you had to use more than two numbers?*
➤ *What if one number had to be odd?*
➤ *What if one number had to be >2 and <5?*

Can you give me an example of a **Roman** numeral? Another, another, another.
➤ *What if it had to be over 10?*
➤ *What if it had to use the same letter twice?*

Can you give me an example of a ThHTO + ThHTO addition? Another, another, another.
➤ *What if you had to calculate it mentally?*
➤ *What if the answer had to be more than 10 000?*
➤ *What if the answer had to be less than 2 500?*
➤ *What if it had to involve multiples of 4?*

Can you give me an example of a multiplication you can carry out mentally? Another, another, another.
➤ *What if both numbers had to be over 10?*
➤ *What if both numbers had to be over 10, but couldn't be multiples of 10?*

Can you give me an example of a fraction that is equivalent to $\frac{3}{4}$? Another, another, another.
➤ *What if the denominator had to be 12?*
➤ *What if the numerator had to be 8?*

Q Activities and investigations

Child A: We could do 2 000 + 100 + 8.

Child B: Can we change our 2 000 into 1 000? So 1 000 + 1 000 + 100 + 8.

Child A: Yes! We could also change our 1 000 into 500 so 500 + 500 + 500 + 500 + 100 + 8.

Key strategy

Give the children a set of mathematical items (e.g. numbers, shapes or statements) and ask them either to order the items or put them into groups.

Why it's effective

This strategy encourages children to think about the properties of the items they are given and to reason about them. It encourages children to make links between items and areas of maths and to consider how they are related.

Tips for use

Initially, ask children to order or group the items in one way. Once they have ordered or grouped the items, ask them to try to find another way of grouping the items.

Whilst some items (e.g. decimal numbers) could be both ordered and grouped, others (e.g. 3-D shapes) may only be grouped. The activity works best with items that could be grouped or ordered in more than one way. For many questions using this strategy, children may find ordering the items helpful when asked to group them, or grouping the items useful when being asked to order them.

You can focus the use of this strategy by introducing additional instructions (e.g. *Can you order the angles based on their size? Can you group the shapes by the number of lines of symmetry they have?*). However, it is important to ensure that the additional instructions do not remove all elements of reasoning from the activity.

This strategy can be used in conjunction with other key strategies in this book. 'What's the same, what's different?' can be a particularly effective way of helping children analyse the items and begin to group/order them. 'Another, another, another', 'Convince me' and 'What do you notice?' can also work well when combined with this strategy.

It is useful to analyse children's methods for creating their responses – are they grouping/ordering based on the initial 'obvious' response, or are they looking deeper at the connections and relationships between the items?

You should encourage children to make generalisations by focusing on what their responses have in common. Children could be encouraged to discuss and compare their responses with a partner or wider group. It can also be a valuable activity to invite children to create their own 'Can you arrange … ?' style problems.

The activity can be extended further by asking children how many possible groups or orders there are, or by asking them to convince you that their group or order is the 'best'. This is especially interesting if there are children who have ordered or grouped the items in different ways. In addition, it can be interesting to discuss any items that could be classified into more than one group.

Watch out

Children may stick to one way of ordering/grouping.

Children may only see one way of ordering/grouping the items. Asking probing questions about certain items of the set and the use of the 'What's the same, what's different?' strategy can help children to see different connections and different ways of ordering/grouping the items.

Try these

Here are some examples to introduce your class to this strategy. In these examples, the content level is sometimes lower than that set out in the National Curriculum for Year 4. This is to allow children to focus on the development of reasoning skills, without being restricted by subject knowledge.

Arrange 1432, 3567, 307, 109, 288, 2017 into two groups.
Possible groups:
➤ Odd and even numbers
➤ Numbers more than 2000 and numbers less than 2000
➤ 3-digit numbers and 4-digit numbers

Arrange 5 × 6 = 30, 3 × 7 = 21, 6 × 5 = 30, 6 + 6 + 6 + 6 + 6 = 30, 7 + 7 + 7 = 21, 21 ÷ 3 = 7 into two groups.
Possible groups:
➤ Related facts:
  ● 5 × 6 = 30, 6 × 5 = 30, 6 + 6 + 6 + 6 + 6 = 30
  ● 3 × 7 = 21, 7 + 7 + 7 = 21, 21 ÷ 3 = 7

Arrange 10, −3, 3, −5, 8, 0, 5 into an order.
Possible orders:
➤ Order of size from smallest to largest: (−5, −3, 0, 5, 8, 10)
➤ Order of size from largest to smallest: (10, 8, 5, 0, −3, −5)

Arrange 15, 12, 18, 21, 34, 20 into groups.
Possible groups:
➤ Numbers with four factors and numbers with six factors
➤ Numbers with two factor pairs and numbers with three factor pairs

Arrange four o'clock, ten to nine in the evening,

20:48 , 21:11 **into groups/into an order.**

Possible order:

➤ , four o'clock,   , 20:48 ,

ten to nine in the evening, 21:11

Possible groups:
➤ Time in words and time on clocks
➤ Times on an analogue clock and times on a digital clock
➤ 24-hour clock times and 12-hour clock times

Arrange these into two groups:

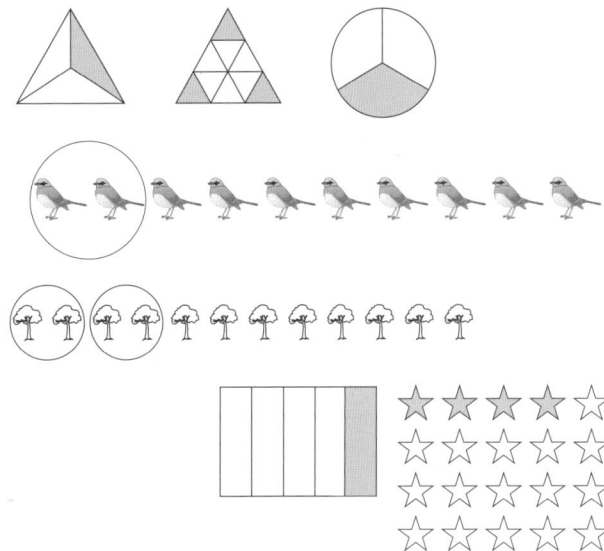

Possible groups:
➤ $\frac{1}{3}$ and $\frac{1}{5}$ representations
➤ Fractions of objects and fractions of shapes

🔍 Activities and investigations

4 Making 28
12 Sequences of signs

4 Convince me

Key strategy

Give the children a statement and ask them to decide whether it is accurate or not, and then to explain their reasoning to convince you.

Why it's effective

This key strategy encourages children to look at the structure of mathematics and is another way for them to explore the concept of mathematical proof. Through trying to convince someone that a statement is true, children will begin to make generalisations and develop their algebraic thinking.

Tips for use

This strategy is particularly effective when the statements given to children are statements which they take for granted and assume are correct. Asking children to convince you that they are true (e.g. multiplication is commutative, i.e. $a \times b = b \times a$) will deepen their conceptual understanding.

Whilst the strategy can be effectively used with given statements, perhaps the most powerful use of this strategy is in response to children's own statements. This can sometimes lead to an impromptu, but valuable, diversion from the planned activity.

The strategy can be used alongside the 'Always, sometimes, never' strategy to help develop and prompt children's thinking.

When supporting children in responding to this strategy, the following USE ME stages are often useful (see the 'Problem-solving techniques' section for more detail):

➤ **Understanding:** do children understand the statement?
➤ **Specialising:** looking at one or a small number of examples of the statement.
➤ **Encouraging representations:** *how could we represent the statement, or our specific examples of the statement?*
➤ **Making generalisations:** *by looking at our specialised examples, can we begin to make a statement that applies to all examples?*
➤ **Extending:** provide a further, linked, question for children to explore. This often works well when used with other strategies from this book.

Watch out

Children may respond with 'Because it is … '.

When children are first asked to convince someone that a statement is true, they often reply with a response along the lines of 'Because it is … ' or 'Because my teachers have always told me'. They can be encouraged to respond in the form 'It is true that ... because ... '.

Children may not know where to start.

First check if children have the required prior knowledge and understanding to be able to convince you that the statement is true. If they do, then providing some initial probing questions, perhaps in 'panic envelopes' (see the 'Problem-solving techniques' section for more detail) can help them to follow a line of reasoning.

Case studies from the classroom

A snippet from a conversation between two Year 4 children discussing this question: *Can you convince me that multiplication is commutative?*

Try these

Here are some examples to introduce your class to this strategy. In these examples, the content level is sometimes lower than that set out in the National Curriculum for Year 4. This is to allow children to focus on the development of reasoning skills, without being restricted by subject knowledge.

Convince me ... that addition is commutative.
➤ (Understanding) *What does commutative mean?*
➤ (Specialising) *Let's look at an example. Is 214 + 32 the same as 32 + 214?*
➤ (Encouraging representations) *How could we represent an addition? Does this help us show it can be done in either order?*
➤ (Making generalisations) *Would this be the same for any addition facts?*
➤ (Extending) *Are there any other operations that are commutative?*

Convince me ... that multiples of 8 are also multiples of 4.
➤ (Understanding) *What does multiple mean?*
➤ (Specialising) *Can we list some multiples of 8? Are these multiples of 4?*
➤ (Encouraging representations) *Could we present multiples of 8 and 4 on a 100 square? What do you notice?*
➤ (Making generalisations) *Are all multiples of 8 multiples of 4?*
➤ (Extending) *Can you think of any other numbers whose multiples would also all be multiples of 4?*

Convince me ... that the product of an odd and an even number is always even.
➤ (Understanding) *What does product mean?*
➤ (Specialising) *Think of some odd and even numbers to multiply together. Are their products even?*

➤ (Encouraging representations) *Could we represent our multiplications using number blocks or on a number line? Does this help us understand why this might be the case?*
➤ (Making generalisations) *Is the product of any pair of odd and even numbers always even?*
➤ (Extending) *What do you think the product of two even numbers would always be? Why? How about the product of two odd numbers?*

Convince me ... that, when you add fractions with the same denominator, the denominator doesn't change.
➤ (Understanding) *What does denominator mean?*
➤ (Specialising) *Can we think of an example of a fraction addition to test this out?*
➤ (Encouraging representations) *How could we represent our fraction additions? Could we use fraction strips or blocks?*
➤ (Making generalisations) *Why might this always be the case?*
➤ (Extending) *What about if we subtract fractions with the same denominator?*

Activities and investigations

Child A: It's true because, if you have two questions with the same numbers, like 6 × 4 and 4 × 6, they both come up with the same anwer.

Child B: And in the times table grid, there are two times tables with the same answer.

Child A: What do you mean?

Child B: Well, if you find 4 across the top and 8 down the side, the answer is 32, and if you do it the other way, find 8 at the top and 4 at the side, it's still 32.

5 Give me an example

Key strategy

Give the children a mathematical statement or criteria (e.g. a fraction equivalent to $\frac{1}{2}$) and ask them to give you examples that meet this statement.

Why it's effective

This strategy encourages children to find specific examples which meet a given statement or criteria. By asking children to provide examples of a statement/criteria given by the teacher or another child, you are encouraging them to develop their skills of specialising, that is, finding specific examples of a generalised statement. This strategy also provides an ideal opportunity to assess children's theoretical understanding of a concept or area in mathematics.

Tips for use

Initially give the statement/criteria and ask children to find you an example that meets it. If needed, additional prompt questions can be asked (see 'Try these' for examples). Giving these further prompt questions can also help to explore children's theoretical understanding of a concept.

Statements/criteria can be made more specific by introducing additional constraints (e.g. *Give me an example of an odd multiple of 17.*).

This strategy can be used in conjunction with other key strategies in this book, including 'Another, another, another' and 'Strange and obvious'.

'Give me an example' can also be combined with the 'Convince me' strategy, with children being asked to convince you that their answer meets the statement or criteria that has been set.

The activity can be extended further by asking children to compare their answers with each other and, if there is a range of answers, asking them *What's the same, what's different?* and then, depending on the criteria set, asking them to come up with a rule/generalised statement that applies to all of their answers.

Watch out

Children may jump to an obvious, or the first, example.

When children are asked to give an example of a statement/criteria, they often respond with the first answer that comes to them. You can address this by being more specific with the criteria/statement given, or by the use of the 'Another, another, another' strategy. You could also ask children to give you an example, but not to give you the first answer that they think of (e.g. *Give me an example of … Great, hold that answer in your head. Can you find another answer?*).

Try these

Here are some examples to introduce your class to this strategy. In these examples, the content level is sometimes lower than that set out in the National Curriculum for Year 4. This is to allow children to focus on the development of reasoning skills, without being restricted by subject knowledge.

Give me an example of a way of partitioning 1673 that includes the number 12.
Prompt questions:
➤ *What does partitioning mean?*
➤ *Do we just have to partition into hundreds, tens and ones?*

Give me an example of a shape which contains at least two obtuse angles.
Prompt questions:
➤ *What does obtuse mean?*
➤ *What shapes can we think of?*
➤ *Can you draw a shape that only has obtuse angles? Why? Why not?*

Give me an example of a multiple of 25.
Prompt questions:
➤ *What does multiple mean?*
➤ *What patterns do we notice about multiples of 25?*

Give me an example of a number you would say when you count in nines from 0.
Prompt questions:
➤ *Could you mark the numbers you say when you count in nines on a 100 square?*
➤ *What do you notice?*
➤ *What do you notice about the sum of the digits in multiples of 9?*

Give me an example of an operation that is commutative.
Prompt questions:
➤ *What does commutative mean?*
➤ *Does it matter in which order you do addition/ multiplication?*
➤ *How could we check this?*

Give me an example of a way of showing $\frac{3}{8}$.
Prompt questions:
➤ *What does a fraction mean?*
➤ *What does $\frac{3}{8}$ mean?*
➤ *Do all the sections/groups need to be an equal size/number?*

Give me an example of a question, in words, that involves division and money.
Prompt question:
➤ *When do we use division each day?*

Give me an example of two 24-hour clock times with an interval of 45 minutes.
Prompt question:
➤ *What does interval mean?*

Give me an example of a way to find the perimeter of our playground.
Prompt questions:
➤ *What units would we measure in?*
➤ *Do we have to measure all sides?*

Activities and investigations

1 The Queen's lawn mower
3 The curious postman
7 Delivery drones
9 It's a fraction of feet
17 Revenge of the creepers

6 Hard and easy

Key strategy

Ask the children to give you an example of a 'hard' and 'easy' answer to a question, explaining why one is 'hard' and the other 'easy'.

Why it's effective

This strategy encourages children to think closely about the structure of mathematics and enables them to demonstrate a theoretical understanding of concepts. Children enjoy the challenge of coming up with 'hard' examples that still meet the requirements set out in the question.

The choices children make when responding to this strategy often provide valuable information about what they find difficult, which may not always be what you expect! For example, if a child constantly gives calculations involving decimals as 'hard' questions, then this would probably indicate they are insecure with decimal place value.

Tips for use

Unlike most of the strategies in this book, this strategy generally works best if children are encouraged to respond individually first. Once they have come up with their own 'hard' and 'easy' responses they should then be encouraged to discuss and compare these with a partner or larger group. The strategy 'What's the same, what's different?' can be used here to encourage children to compare and contrast their responses and draw out key themes/concepts.

Children should be encouraged to explain why the examples they have given are 'hard' or 'easy'. This could be by way of a written explanation or by verbally convincing their partner/an adult that their responses are 'hard' or 'easy'.

Watch out

Children may respond to the request for a 'hard' example by giving very large multiples of 10 (e.g. 46 000 + 20 000).

Ask children to convince you why this is a 'hard' example. Then discuss how this could be made 'easy', e.g. by multiplying/dividing by a multiple of 10 and using known facts (in the example above, $46 + 20 = 66$, $66 \times 1\,000 = 66\,000$).

Try these

Here are some examples to introduce your class to this strategy. In these examples, the content level is sometimes lower than that set out in the National Curriculum for Year 4. This is to allow children to focus on the development of reasoning skills, without being restricted by subject knowledge.

Give me a hard and easy example of an addition number sentence that you would need to use a written method for.
➤ Easy: $46 + 27 =$ as it is only two digits and only one of the places crosses the tens boundary
➤ Hard: $8\,975 + 9\,946 =$ as all of the places cross the tens boundaries and therefore an exchange would need to take place four times

Give me a hard and easy example of a subtraction number sentence that you would need to use a written method for.
➤ Easy: $63 - 43 =$ as it is only two digits and none of the places would involve exchanging
➤ Hard: $9\,346 - 8\,438 =$ as it is four digits and two of the places would involve exchanging

Case studies from the classroom

A snippet from a conversation between two Year 4 children discussing this question: *Give me a hard and an easy example of a multiple of 6 that is more than 100.*

Give me a hard and easy example of a way to partition 7563.

➤ Easy: 7000 + 500 + 60 + 3 as it is partitioned along the thousands, hundreds, tens and ones boundary (canonically)

➤ Hard: 96 + 169 + 5642 + 652 + 6 + 589 + 409 as it is partitioned into seven numbers, none of which are 'obvious' within 7563

Give me a hard and easy example of a fraction equivalent to $\frac{6}{7}$.

➤ Easy: $\frac{12}{14}$ as we have just doubled the numerator and denominator

➤ Hard: $\frac{168}{196}$ as it is not immediately clear that 168 is a multiple of 12 and 196 is a multiple of 14

Give me a hard and easy example of a number to multiply by 100.

➤ Easy: 870 as it is a multiple of 10
➤ Hard: 75.32 as it is a decimal number

Give me a hard and easy example of a division question.

➤ Easy: 12 ÷ 4 = as 12 is a low multiple of 4
➤ Hard: 673 ÷ 7 as it would involve a written method

Give me a hard and easy example of a number to find 1000 less than.

➤ Easy: 1056 as it only contains one thousand
➤ Hard: 10323 as it will involve crossing a thousands boundary

Give me a hard and easy example of a fraction addition sentence.

➤ Easy: $\frac{1}{7} + \frac{2}{7}$ as the answer is below 1 so it will be a proper fraction

➤ Hard: $\frac{3}{7} + \frac{2}{7} + \frac{1}{7}$ as it has three fractions to add

Give me a hard and easy example of a two-step word problem.

➤ Easy: any one-operation two-step word problem as it only involves one operation

➤ Hard: any two-operation two-step word problem as it involves two operations

Give me a hard and easy example of a rectilinear shape to find the area of by counting the squares.

➤ Easy:

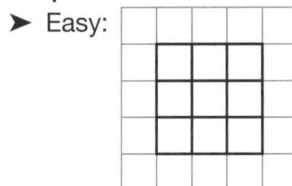

as it is a square so it is easy to count

➤ Hard:

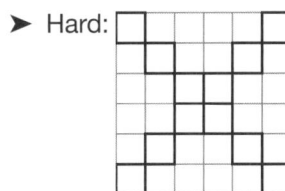

as it is not a simple rectangle and has lots of sections to count

Activities and investigations

6 Crayon boxes
8 Money mix-up
13 Mixed-up offers
14 Mr Shah's swimming pool shambles
15 Mission multiply

Child A: Well, an easy example would be 600, as that's a multiple of 6 and 100.

Child B: A more difficult one would be something like 390, as it takes a bit of work to prove it's a multiple of 6. But it is, as we know than 300 is a multiple of 6, and 90 is as well, so 390 must be!

Key strategy

Give the children an answer and ask them to come up with as many questions as possible that could have that answer.

Why it's effective

This strategy encourages children to think creatively and explore the structure of the numbers and mathematics. Children will begin to spot and use patterns and through this make their own generalisations.

Tips for use

Children should be encouraged to share their possible questions in pairs and collate them together, explaining their possible questions to their partner if needed. Finally, each pair could be invited to share a possible question with the class, picking a question which they think no one else will have come up with. This provides a great opportunity for further questioning, which could incorporate some of the other key strategies, such as 'Convince me', 'Always, sometimes, never' and 'Another, another, another'.

Recording possible questions on a mind map, with the answer in the middle, is an effective way to record responses to this key strategy. Online collective canvases such as lino-it (www.linoit.com) and padlet (www.padlet.com) can also be effective to collaboratively record possible answers.

Children can be encouraged to put their possible questions into categories. Some obvious categories could be questions related to multiplication, questions which involve an even number, questions which are in context, etc. However, asking children to categorise their possible questions themselves is often surprising and creates a good opportunity for further discussion.

The strategy can also be easily differentiated by adding set criteria to challenge or support children, e.g. only questions that involve negative numbers, only questions that involve multiplication, etc.

The strategy provides a great opportunity to encourage children to follow patterns. For example, if a suggested question is 4×8, can they see that 2×16, 1×32 and 0.5 of 64 are also possible questions?

Finally, the strategy can work well if it is run as a timed competition. Set a time limit and challenge children to come up with as many possible questions as they can, before then going through some of the follow-up stages suggested above.

Watch out

Children may get stuck with one rule.

Sometimes children will get stuck with one 'rule' or type of question, e.g. addition questions. This can easily be overcome by asking the child to make their next question different: *What about a question involving a fraction? Give me a question involving a negative number.*

Case studies from the classroom

A snippet from a conversation between two Year 4 children discussing this question:
If the answer is 36, what could the possible question be?

Try these

Here are some examples to introduce your class to this strategy. In these examples, the content level is sometimes lower than that set out in the National Curriculum for Year 4. This is to allow children to focus on the development of reasoning skills, without being restricted by subject knowledge.

If the answer is 2 000, what could the possible questions be?
➤ Challenge: *One of your questions must include multiplication.*

If the answer is 20, what could the possible questions be?
➤ Challenge: *One of your questions must include a division.*

If the answer is 7, 14, 21, what could the possible questions be?
➤ Challenge: *One of your questions must involve properties of numbers.*

If the answer is a number ≤ 1 000, what could the possible questions be?
➤ Challenge: *One of your questions must include a calculation.*

If the answer is 14 monkeys, what could the possible questions be?
➤ Challenge: *One of your questions must involve a non-unit fraction.*

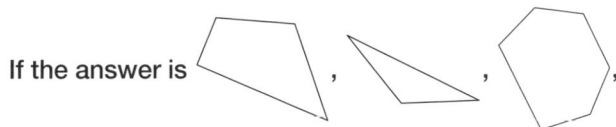

If the answer is , , ,

what could the possible question be?
➤ Challenge: *Your question must involve the word, 'angle'.*

If the answer is 891, what could the possible questions be?
➤ Challenge: *One of your questions must involve the subtraction of two 4-digit numbers.*

If the answer is –4, what could the possible questions be?
➤ Challenge: *One of your questions must involve counting backwards.*

If the answer is £3.48, what could the possible questions be?
➤ Challenge: *one of your questions must involve a subtraction that you can carry out mentally.*

If the answer is eight factors, what could the possible questions be?
➤ Challenge: *One of your questions must involve a number larger than 40.*

Activities and investigations

3 The curious postman
8 Money mix-up
18 Pole position

Child A: It could be 26 + 10 = ?

Child B: Or 27 + 9 = ?

Child A: We could follow a pattern then: 28 + 8 = ?, 29 + 7 = ?, 30 + 6 = ?, 31 + 5 = ? ...

💡 Key strategy

Give the children a number, geometry concept or measure and ask them to write its 'story', that is, as much as they know or can work out about it.

Why it's effective

This strategy encourages children to explore everything they know about a mathematical concept and is therefore particularly effective at developing children's subject knowledge whilst also encouraging them to reason.

Through telling a 'story', children are also likely to form and use their own generalisations and patterns, which can be a great starting point for further discussion.

Tips for use

Start by giving children a number (which could include a decimal, a fraction, a multiple of 100, etc.), a geometry concept (e.g. a shape or co-ordinate) or a measure (e.g. an angle). Then ask them to write as many statements as they can about the item given.

For example, when given a number, children may choose to look at the classification of the number (odd, even, square, etc.), the factors and multiples of the number, doubling and halving the number, sums and differences that lead to the number, or statements that involve proportions of the number, etc.

As children create their 'story' they are likely to create and use their own generalisations and patterns. Discussing these with children using the 'What else do we know?' and 'What do we notice?' key strategies is particularly effective.

This strategy can also work well as an individual or paired activity, followed by a class 'race' to record as many different elements of the number 'story' as possible on an interactive whiteboard within a given time limit.

Watch out

! Children may focus on one pattern.

Children often get 'locked on' to one pattern, e.g. doubling and halving. Encourage children to explore other patterns by setting a target number of 'unrelated' facts to record.

! Children may 'run out' of facts to record.

Sometimes children will appear to run out of facts to record. Draw children's attention to patterns within what they have recorded so far and ask: *What else do we know?* A bank of prompt questions may also be useful, e.g. *What number is double the number? What are the factors of the number?*

Try these

Here are some examples to introduce your class to this strategy. In these examples, the content level is sometimes lower than that set out in the National Curriculum for Year 4. This is to allow children to focus on the development of reasoning skills, without being restricted by subject knowledge.

General prompt questions to use with number-based stories
➤ *What type of number is it?*
➤ *What is it a multiple of?*

Case studies from the classroom

A snippet from a conversation between two Year 4 children discussing this question: *What is the story of 22?*

- ➤ *What are some multiples of the number?*
- ➤ *What factors does it have? Does this mean it is a special type of number?*
- ➤ *Can you write this as a fraction/decimal/ percentage?*
- ➤ *What is double the number? Double this number?*
- ➤ *What is half the number? Half this number?*
- ➤ *Can you round this number to the nearest 10/100/1 000?*
- ➤ *What happens when you multiply the number by 100? 1 000?*

- ➤ *What happens when you divide the number by 10? 100?*
- ➤ *What can you add together to make this number?*
- ➤ *What calculations could this number be involved in?*

Activities and investigations

13 Mixed-up offers

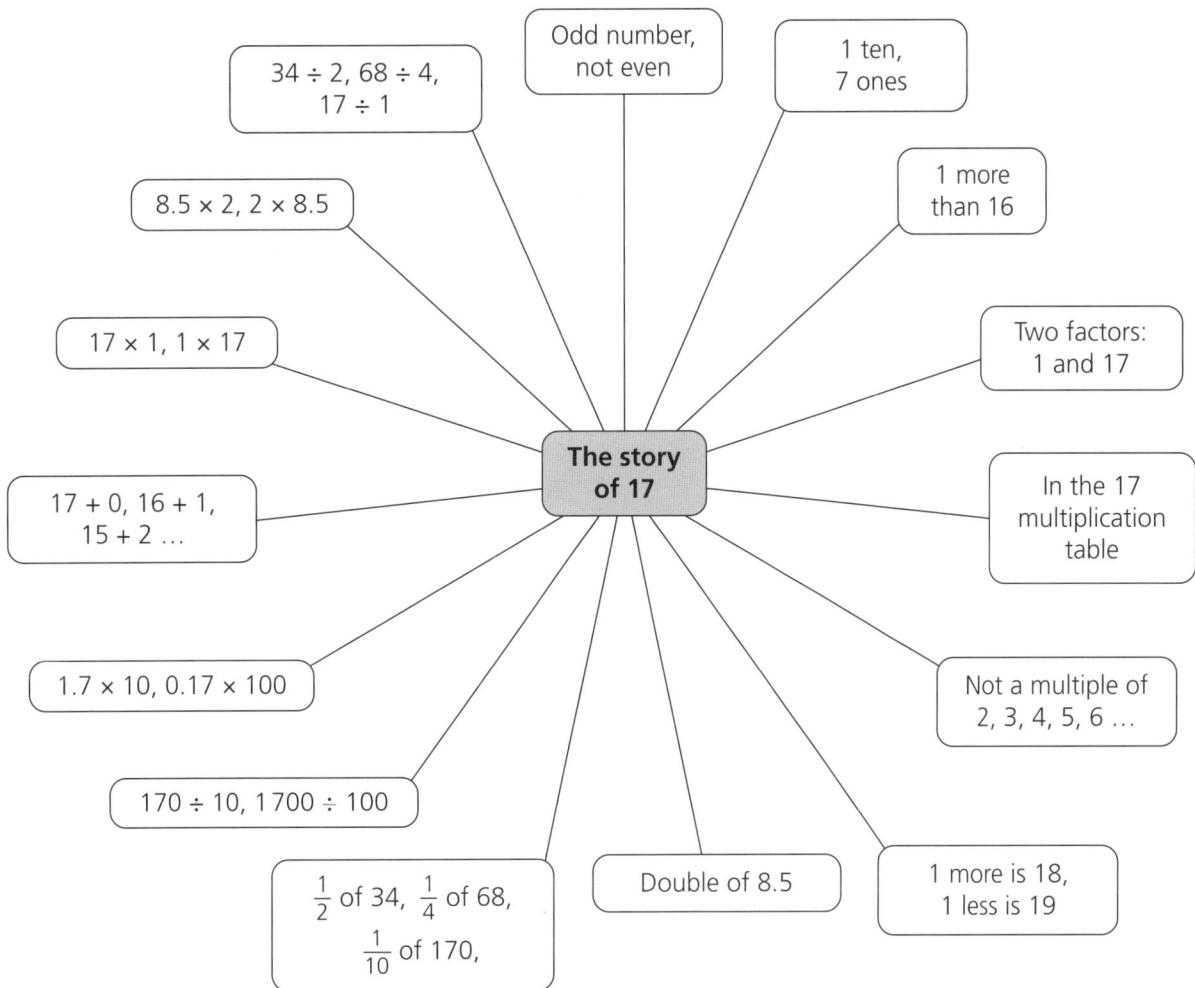

34 ÷ 2, 68 ÷ 4, 17 ÷ 1

Odd number, not even

1 ten, 7 ones

8.5 × 2, 2 × 8.5

1 more than 16

17 × 1, 1 × 17

Two factors: 1 and 17

The story of 17

17 + 0, 16 + 1, 15 + 2 …

In the 17 multiplication table

1.7 × 10, 0.17 × 100

Not a multiple of 2, 3, 4, 5, 6 …

170 ÷ 10, 1 700 ÷ 100

$\frac{1}{2}$ of 34, $\frac{1}{4}$ of 68, $\frac{1}{10}$ of 170,

Double of 8.5

1 more is 18, 1 less is 19

Child A: 22 is a number, and it's even.

Child B: It's half of 44.

Child A: Which must also mean it's a quarter of 88.

9 Odd one out

💡 Key strategy

Give the children a set of three or more numbers or statements and ask them to identify which number/statement is the odd one out and why.

Why it's effective

When children work to identify the odd one out, they will be conjecturing and reasoning about the items in the set. Almost without realising it, they will create their own generalisations and test all parts of the set given to them against this to try to identify the odd one out.

Tips for use

This strategy works particularly well when there is time for paired or grouped discussion, with children attempting to convince each other which item from the set is the odd one out.

To further increase the reasoning required, especially when children have had some experience responding to this strategy, always aim to choose the set of numbers/statements you provide so that there is more than one possible answer. This can create a good debate in the classroom, with different children trying to convince each other that the number they have selected is the 'real' odd one out.

This strategy could also be combined with the 'Another, another, another' strategy, by asking children to generate further examples that would either be similar to the odd one out or to the rest of the set.

Watch out

! **Children may not see the link between parts of the set.**

Sometimes children will struggle to find the odd one out as they cannot spot the generalities (links) between different parts of the set. Focusing children's thinking using the 'What's the same, what's different?' key strategy, initially with pairs from the set, can help children see the similarities and differences between parts of the set. Using 'panic envelopes' (see the 'Problem-solving techniques' section for more detail) containing key questions to focus thinking can also be effective in supporting children to see the link between parts of the set.

Try these

Here are some examples to introduce your class to this strategy. In these examples, the content level is sometimes lower than that set out in the National Curriculum for Year 4. This is to allow children to focus on the development of reasoning skills, without being restricted by subject knowledge.

Look at this set of numbers: 23, 166, 115, 150. Which is the odd one out and why?
Possible odd ones out with reasons:
➤ 23 as it is the only number with just two factors
➤ 115 as it is the only odd number above 100
➤ 115 as it is the only number which rounds to 100 when rounded to the nearest 100

Case studies from the classroom

A snippet from a conversation between two Year 4 children discussing this question:
Look at 6 × 10 = ?, 0.6 ×10 = ? or 60 × 10 = ? Which is the odd one out?

Look at these number sentences: $3 - 4 = ?$, $779 \times 0 = ?$, $904 + ? = 2000$, double $702 = ?$
Which is the odd one out and why?
Possible odd ones out with reasons:
➤ Double $702 = ?$ as it is the only number sentence that involves a double
➤ $904 + ? = 2000$ as it is the only number sentence which doesn't have an unknown total or difference at the end
➤ $779 \times 0 = ?$ as it is the only number sentence that has an answer of 0
➤ $3 - 4 = ?$ as it is the only number sentence which has a negative number as an answer

Look at these shapes:

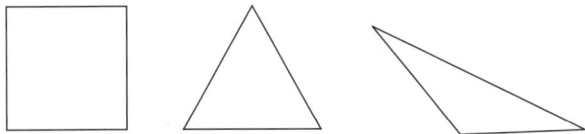

Which is the odd one out and why?
Possible odd ones out with reasons:
➤ The scalene triangle as it is the only one whose sides are not all the same length
➤ The scalene triangle as it is the only one which contains an obtuse angle
➤ The square as it is the only one with four right angles

Look at these numbers: 64, 160, 8015, 62. **Which is the odd one out and why?**
Possible odd ones out with reasons:
➤ 62 as it is the only number which isn't a multiple of 8
➤ 160 as it is the only number which is a multiple of 10
➤ 8015 as it is the only number bigger than 1000
➤ 64 as it is the only number with an odd number of factors

Look at these fractions: $\frac{3}{15}$, $\frac{6}{15}$, $\frac{20}{50}$, $\frac{10}{25}$. **Which is the odd one out and why?**
Possible odd one out with reason:
➤ $\frac{3}{15}$ as it is the only fraction which is not equivalent to $\frac{2}{5}$

Activities and investigations

3   The curious postman
17 Revenge of the creepers

Child A: 6 is the odd one out, because it is the only number without a 0.

Child B: But is 0.6×10 the odd one out? Because it is the only one that doesn't have a 0 in the answer, it isn't a 10 or a 100. It is also the odd one out because it is the only one to have a 0 before you times it.

10 Strange and obvious

Key strategy

Ask the children to give a strange, an obvious example and, if they are able, a general example of a statement.

Why it's effective

This key strategy encourages children to think about the structure of mathematics and the definition of the statements given. Through focusing on what makes a strange or obvious example of a given statement, children have to think carefully about the statement given, the criteria needed to meet the statement and what examples they could give. The encouragement to give a strange example encourages children to push the boundaries of their understanding, whilst the general example encourages them to begin to develop algebraic thinking.

Tips for use

This key strategy could be used either as part of shared learning, as the main activity in the lesson or as an effective plenary. Children should be encouraged to explain their choices, either verbally or in writing, which will encourage them to think about the definition of the given statement and the general structure of mathematics. The strategy works particularly well if children are encouraged to discuss and convince each other that their examples fit with the statement and are strange, obvious or, for some questions, general. When working in pairs, children can also be encouraged to think of reasons why their partner's responses may not be strange or obvious (or general).

Encourage children to first state and then record an **obvious** example. *What is the first example you think of? Why is this the first example that you think of?* They can always replace their obvious example with a 'more obvious' example whilst they are thinking through the activity.

Then ask children to think of their **strange** example. Encourage them to think about the definition and criteria of the statement given. *What fits our definition but isn't obvious?*

Finally, children should be encouraged to think about a **general** example. This will deepen their thinking about the statement given and their understanding. It could be extended to a basic algebraic statement.

Depending on the desired outcomes and ability of children to reason, the requirement for a general example could be skipped.

Watch out

! **Children may rush to give a really big or small number.**

In numerical questions, children will often state a really large or small number which they arrive at by multiplying or dividing by 10, 100, 1 000, etc. as their strange example. Discuss with children if, just because an example is really large or small, it is strange. *What makes it strange? Is it really quite obvious as all we have done is multiplied/divided by a large number?* You can also modify the question to remove the temptation to go really large (e.g. *Can you give me a strange example of an odd number that is below 50?*).

! **Children's general statements are not general.**

Using the strategy 'Always, sometimes, never' to encourage children to check their general statements can help them ensure their statements are truly general.

Case studies from the classroom

A snippet from a conversation between two Year 4 children discussing this question: *Give me a strange, obvious and general example of a multiple of 9.*

Try these

Here are some examples to introduce your class to this strategy. In these examples, the content level is sometimes lower than that set out in the National Curriculum for Year 4. This is to allow children to focus on the development of reasoning skills, without being restricted by subject knowledge.

Give me a strange, obvious and general example of an even number over 9120.

➤ Strange: 44 444 as it involves all of the same digits. *How do you know it's even?*
➤ Obvious: 9122 as it is the first even number above 9120. *What is the tenth even number above 9120?*
➤ General: a number that is more than 9120 and ends in the digits 0, 2, 4, 6, 8

Give me a strange, obvious and general example of a subtraction number sentence.

➤ Strange: $1987 - 50 - 8 = ?$ as it has three numbers in it, so it involves subtracting two numbers. *How would you work out the answer to this?*
➤ Obvious: $3 - 2 = 1$ as it is a basic subtraction
➤ General: a number sentence where you are finding the difference between two or more numbers, or where you are subtracting one or more numbers (which are usually smaller) from another number

Give me a strange, obvious and general example of a multiple of 7.

➤ Strange: 749 as it is a high multiple of 7. *How do you know it is still a multiple of 7?*
➤ Obvious: 7 as it is the first multiple of 7
➤ General: any number which you would say if you continued to count in sevens from 0

Give me a strange, obvious and general example of a way of showing $\frac{5}{9}$ of a shape.

➤ Strange:

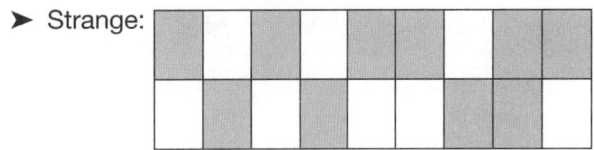

as it is split into more than 9 sections and the shaded parts aren't all together. *How do you know it is still showing $\frac{5}{9}$?*

➤ Obvious:

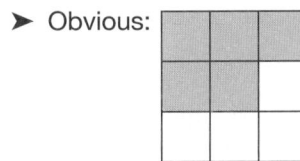

as it is split into 9 sections and 5 of them are shaded

➤ General: any shape split into equal sections that are a multiple of 9, where 5 out of each 9 are shaded

Give me a strange, obvious and general example of a shape with two obtuse angles.

Give me a strange, obvious and general example of a fraction subtraction.

Give me a strange, obvious and general example of a number with an odd number of factors.

Give me a strange, obvious and general example of a shape with a perimeter of 12 cm.

Give me a strange, obvious and general example of a shape with an area of 15 squares.

Give me a strange, obvious and general example of two numbers with a sum of 6730.

Activities and investigations

6 Crayon boxes
12 Sequences of signs

Child A: 9 is obvious, as it's the first multiple!

Child B: A strange one would be one where it's not immediately obvious it's a multiple of 9, like 504.

Child A: General would be any number which divides by 9 without leaving a remainder.

💡 Key strategy

Ask the children to give you a 'silly' answer to a question and to explain why it is a silly answer.

Why it's effective

By asking children to give you a silly answer to a question they will have to reason about the range into which the possible correct answers could fall. This will require them to consider the properties that the question entails and will involve them in making a generalisation about the correct answer(s) in order to explain why their answer is silly.

Tips for use

Always ensure you ask children to justify their silly answer and explain why it can't possibly be a correct answer.

Children can also be asked to create a number of silly answers and then to order them by silliness. Encourage them to identify which silly answer is close to the real answer or involves a common error/misconception. This can be a great way to address misconceptions with children.

Modifiers can also be added to the base question to restrict the range of possible silly answers. Depending on the restrictions added, this can prompt deeper thinking and reasoning.

This strategy works well when children are given the opportunity to discuss their silly answer(s) and reasons why they are silly. The strategy 'What's the same, what's different?' can be used to encourage

children to compare, contrast and look for links between their silly answers.

Watch out

❗ Children may always give very large answers.

Children's natural instinct when asked for a silly answer is often to go for a very large answer (e.g. 4 trillion, infinity, etc.). Depending on the question given, either ask children if they can prove that this is not an answer to the question (particularly interesting when the question relates to a statement, rather than a calculation) or place a restriction on the range of answers allowed.

Try these

Here are some examples to introduce your class to this strategy. In these examples, the content level is sometimes lower than that set out in the National Curriculum for Year 4. This is to allow children to focus on the development of reasoning skills, without being restricted by subject knowledge.

Give me a silly answer for a number bond to 10 000.
Prompt question:
➤ *What does a number bond mean?*

Example silly answers and justification:
➤ $10015 + 112$: this involves a number above 10000
➤ $500 + 500$: this is clearly a number bond to 1000. *How could you turn this into a number bond to 10 000?*

Give me a silly answer for $13431 - 1832 = ?$
Prompt question:
➤ *How do we work out the answer to a subtraction number sentence?*

Example silly answers and justification:
➤ 14000: this is above 13431 and when you subtract the answer is usually smaller
➤ 0: you aren't taking away 13431 from 13431 so you will have something left

📎 Case studies from the classroom

A snippet from a conversation between two Year 4 children discussing this question: *Give me a silly answer for a calculation involving 196.*

Give me a silly answer for a multiple of 8.
Prompt question:
➤ *How do we find multiples of 8?*

Example silly answers and justification:
➤ 101: it is an odd number and 8 only has even multiples
➤ 7: it is less than 8 and multiples of a number are always greater than the number

Give me a silly answer for a drawing of an obtuse angle.
Prompt questions:
➤ *What does the word 'obtuse' mean?*
➤ *What does the word 'angle' mean?*

Example silly answers and justification:
➤ as this is clearly a right angle

➤ as it is clearly much smaller than a right angle and therefore cannot be an obtuse angle

Give me a silly answer for the perimeter of this shape.

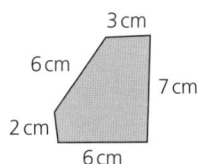

Not to scale

Prompt questions:
➤ *What does perimeter mean?*
➤ *How do we find the perimeter?*

Example silly answers and justification:
➤ 3 cm: it is just the length of one side and the perimeter will always be bigger than the length of one side
➤ 201 cm: it is much larger than 3 + 7 + 6 + 2 + 6
➤ 24 m: the units are different

Give me a silly answer for an equivalent fraction to $\frac{3}{7}$.

Prompt questions:
➤ *What does equivalent mean?*
➤ *How do we find equivalent fractions?*

Example silly answers and justification:
➤ $\frac{2}{10}$: 10 is not a multiple of 7
➤ $\frac{5}{7}$: this has the same denominator as $\frac{3}{7}$

Give me a silly answer for a way to partition 3 067.
Prompt question:
➤ *What does partitioning mean?*

Example silly answers and justification:
➤ 3 067 + 1: it already includes 3 067 and when you partition a number you break it down into numbers which make it up
➤ 1 032 + 45: this won't get you anywhere near 3 067. *What other number(s) would need to be part of the partition of 3 067 if 1 032 + 45 were a part of the partition?*

Child A: 196 – 100 would be silly because the answer is 196 and you're taking away more so it can't be the answer so the answer will be smaller.

Child B: 200 – 196, because you're taking away the answer from a number just a bit bigger so it will be a much lower number than 196.

12 What do you notice?

Key strategy

Ask the children 'What do you notice?' about a number, a set of numbers, a shape or a mathematical statement.

Why it's effective

This strategy encourages children to look deeper into the structure of mathematics. Through answering the question 'What do you notice?', children will be making their own generalisations and testing them against specific examples.

Tips for use

This strategy is very effective when children are given time to talk and discuss the statement with a partner or small groups, before feeding back to the class (or larger group) with the expectation that they convince the larger group of what they notice.

When using this strategy, you can provide children with sets of numbers/mathematical objects (e.g. 3, 6, 9, 12; a rectangle, a square, a rhombus) or general statements/properties (e.g. all multiples of 3; *What happens when you multiply by 100?*).

Children's reasoning skills can be further developed by asking follow-up questions or providing follow-up statements once they have responded to the initial 'What do you notice?' question. The strategy 'Always, sometimes, never' often works well as a follow-up to a 'What do you notice?' question as this allows children to further develop their generalisations.

This strategy can also be used alongside many of the other key strategies to help focus children's thinking and reasoning skills.

Watch out

Children may not see the generalities.

Sometimes children will be unable to independently state the generality or generalities relating to the statement which has been given. To help them see the generality, use follow-up questions which could involve some of the other key strategies. 'What's the same, what's different?' is particularly effective here. 'Panic envelopes' with follow-up questions (see the 'Problem-solving techniques' section for more detail) can also be used.

Try these

Here are some examples to introduce your class to this strategy. In these examples, the content level is sometimes lower than that set out in the National Curriculum for Year 4. This is to allow children to focus on the development of reasoning skills, without being restricted by subject knowledge.

What do you notice about the multiples of 9?
- ➤ *Can you list some of the multiples of 9?*
- ➤ *What's the same, what's different about these numbers?*
- ➤ *What do you notice about the sum of the digits in each multiple?*

What do you notice about this set of numbers: 105, 130, 155 … ?
- ➤ *What are you counting in?*
- ➤ *What will the next number in the sequence be?*
- ➤ *What will the tenth number in the sequence be?*

Case studies from the classroom

A snippet from a conversation between two Year 4 children discussing this question: *What do you notice about multiples of 25?*

What do you notice about fractions that are equivalent to $\frac{2}{9}$?

➤ Let's list some equivalent fractions to $\frac{2}{9}$.
➤ What do you notice about the numerators and denominators in these fractions?
➤ What are the denominators all multiples of?

What do you notice about what happens when you divide by 100?

➤ What happens when you divide 720 by 100?
➤ Does the same thing happen if you divide 72 by 100?
➤ Would a place-value grid help you see what is happening?

What do you notice about the perimeter of a regular shape?

➤ Let's draw some regular shapes. Let's measure their perimeters.
➤ What do you notice/know about the side lengths of regular shapes?
➤ What are the lengths of the sides in the shapes you have drawn?
➤ Is there any link between the number of sides and the perimeter of a regular shape?

Activities and investigations

1 The Queen's lawn mower
2 Patterns on digital clocks
4 Making 28
5 A day in the life of a parking space
7 Delivery drones
10 Flower symmetry
12 Sequences of signs
16 The search continues for the perfect planet!
18 Pole position

Child A: The units go up in a pattern: 5, 0, 5, 0, 5, 0.

Child B: Yes, and the last two digits are always 25, 50, 75 or 00.

Child A: Yes, the tens and ones repeat when they get to any new hundred.

13 What else do we know?

Key strategy

Give the children a statement (e.g. $\frac{1}{4}$ of 40 is 10) and ask them what else they know based on this statement.

Why it's effective

This strategy encourages children to see the links that exist in all areas of mathematics. It encourages them to reason and combine other known facts with the statement. This activity works particularly well as a starter or plenary, or as an early-morning challenge.

Tips for use

Provide the statement and allow children to record everything else they know. Adding a time and/or quantity challenge (e.g. *Can you state at least ten other facts in two minutes?*) can help to add an element of competition!

Try asking the whole class to work on a statement individually, then to share their related facts with a partner, then ask each pair to share with the class a related fact that they think no one else would have come up with. This approach pushes children to think deeper and go beyond the 'obvious' related facts. A mind map can be a useful tool for recording responses to this strategy, with children recording groups of related facts on each arm of their mind maps.

You can also work with children on the 'automatic' related facts that they should be able to state almost instantaneously, e.g. inverse facts (7 + 13 = 20, 20 − 7 = 13) and multiples of 10 (70 × 8, 7 × 80, etc.).

The strategy can also be used with real-life statements (e.g. *If we know that $\frac{1}{4}$ of a class are boys and there are 24 pupils in the class, what else do we know?*).

The 'Strange and obvious' strategy can also be used alongside 'What else do we know?' to deepen the thinking from this strategy.

Watch out

! Children may 'stall'.

Sometimes children will come up with a few 'obvious' related facts (perhaps using inverses, etc.), but then struggle to see any other related facts. Asking children to discuss ideas together can help overcome this, as can encouraging them to 'combine' related facts.

! Facts/statements may not be related.

Sometimes children will provide facts/statements that appear to have no clear relation to the given statement, but be careful not to say categorically that it is not a related fact. Instead, encourage children to explain how it is related, talking you or another child through the steps they have taken to form this related fact. Analysing untrue 'facts' given by children can also help expose any misconceptions that they may hold.

Case studies from the classroom

A snippet from a conversation between two Year 4 children discussing this question: *If we know that $\frac{1}{4} = \frac{2}{8}$, what else do we know?*

Try these

Here are some examples to introduce your class to this strategy. In these examples, the content level is sometimes lower than that set out in the National Curriculum for Year 4. This is to allow children to focus on the development of reasoning skills, without being restricted by subject knowledge.

If we know that 320 + 410 + 209 = 939, what else do we know?
➤ *Is there a subtraction number sentence linked to this addition number sentence?* (939 – 410 – 320 = 209)
➤ *Can you find another subtraction number sentence that is linked to this addition number sentence? How many can you find?*

If we know that $\frac{3}{9}$ of 27 is 9, what else do we know?
➤ *Is there another fraction that is equal to $\frac{3}{9}$?*

If we know that this is $\frac{2}{7}$ of the set, what else do we know?

➤ *What does this fraction mean?*
➤ *How many groups would there be?*
➤ *How many groups do we have here?*
➤ *How many objects would there be in total?*

If we know that 56 ÷ 7 = 8, what else do we know?
➤ *What is the inverse of division?*
➤ *Can we create two multiplication statements from this one division statement?*

If we know that $\frac{1}{4}$ = 0.25, what else do we know?

If we know that an even number add an even number add an odd number always makes an odd number, what else do we know?

If we know that 1 000 g = 1 kg, what else do we know?

If we know the lengths of the sides of this regular hexagon, what else do we know?

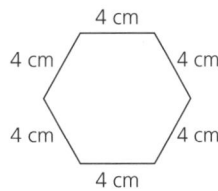

If we know that 0.5 + 0.5 = 1, what else do we know?

If we know that 14, 21, 28, 35 are multiples of 7, what else do we know?

Activities and investigations

Child A: I know that $\frac{1}{4}$ also equals $\frac{2}{8}$.

Child B: I think you can times the top and bottom of the fraction by the same number and it'll still be equal.

Child A: Yes, I think that's right, so we know that $\frac{5}{20}$ and $\frac{8}{32}$ = $\frac{1}{4}$.

Key strategy

Give the children two or more mathematical statements and ask them to find a link between the statements.

Why it's effective

This strategy encourages children to make connections between different areas of mathematics. It encourages them to reason and combine their knowledge of the two or more statements given in order to find the link between them. Careful use of this strategy also helps to show the underlying structure and concepts in mathematics to support the development of a true conceptual understanding.

Tips for use

Initially introduce the two (or more) numbers, statements, objects or concepts and ask children to find the link between them. Using the 'think, pair, share' approach (see the 'Problem-solving techniques' section for more detail) can be very effective with this strategy, as it encourages children to reason about their link and discuss ideas together.

The 'Convince me' strategy can be used alongside this strategy, by asking children to convince you or their partner that the link is correct. You can also ask children to give another number, statement, object or concept that is linked to the ones given, deepening their understanding of the structure of mathematics.

This strategy can be extended by giving numbers, statements or concepts that have multiple possible links, and combining the strategy with 'Another, another, another', asking children to find another link between the numbers, statements, objects or concepts.

Representing the numbers, statements, objects or concepts pictorially or with concrete apparatus can help children to explore the link between them and see the underlying connections in mathematics.

Watch out

Children may 'stall' and get stuck when finding a possible link.

Sometimes children may not be able to find a link, or may only look for and give immediately obvious links. Ask follow-up questions, such as those provided in the 'Try these' section, which help children to explore the underlying structures and concepts.

Try these

Here are some examples to introduce your class to this strategy. In these examples, the content level is sometimes lower than that set out in the National Curriculum for Year 4. This is to allow children to focus on the development of reasoning skills, without being restricted by subject knowledge.

What's the link between the numbers in this sequence: 18, 36, 54, 72, 90?
Prompt questions:
➤ *What does the sequence increase by each time?*
➤ *What would the next two numbers in the sequence be?*
Possible links:
➤ Multiples of 9, or numbers you say when you count in nines from 0
➤ Increase by 18 each time
➤ All even multiples of 9 below 100

What's the link between multiplication and division?
Prompt question:
➤ *If I know a multiplication fact (e.g. 3 × 7 = 21), what else do I know?*
Possible link:
➤ Multiplication is the inverse of division

What's the link between 0.34, 3.4, 34?
Prompt questions:
➤ *What is the link between 3.4 and 34?*
➤ *How is 34 linked to 0.34?*
Possible link:
➤ All are linked by a multiple of 10 (0.34 × 10 = 3.4, 34 ÷ 100 = 0.34, etc.)

What's the link between

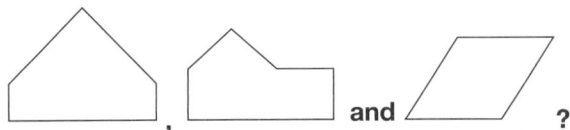

Prompt question:
➤ *What do you notice about the size and classification of the angles in these shapes?*
Possible links:
➤ Shapes are 2-D shapes
➤ All irregular
➤ All have two obtuse angles

What's the link between

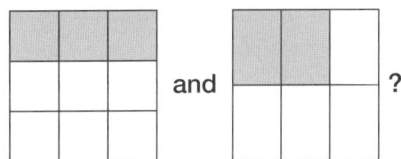

Prompt questions:
➤ *How many sections are there?*
➤ *How many sections are shaded?*
➤ *Do both diagrams show the same fraction?*
Possible links:
➤ Both are ways of showing a fraction of a shape
➤ Both are ways of showing a $\frac{1}{3}$ of a shape as $\frac{3}{9}$ is equal to $\frac{2}{6}$ which both equal $\frac{1}{3}$

What's the link between number bonds to 10 and numbers bonds to 1?
Prompt questions:
➤ *Give me a number bond to 10. What happens if we divide it by 10?*
➤ *Can you find all number bonds to 1 by just using your number bonds to 10?*
Possible link:
➤ You can find some number bonds to 1 by dividing number bonds to 10 by 10

What's the link between 1 032 + 122 = 1 254 and 1 254 − 122 = 1 032?
Prompt questions:
➤ *What do you notice about the two number sentences? Do they contain the same numbers?*
➤ *Is there another number sentence that is missing from this 'set'?*
Possible link:
➤ Inverse operations

What's the link between $\frac{2}{7}$ and $\frac{6}{21}$?
Prompt question:
➤ *Is there another fraction that is equal to $\frac{2}{7}$?*
Possible link:
➤ Both are equivalent fractions

Activities and investigations

2 Patterns on digital clocks
5 A day in the life of a parking space
12 Sequences of signs
14 Mr Shah's swimming pool shambles
17 Revenge of the creepers
18 Pole position

15 What's the same, what's different?

Key strategy

Give the children at least two statements, objects or numbers and ask them to compare them by asking 'What's the same, what's different?'.

Why it's effective

This strategy encourages children to compare and contrast. It fosters children's ability to spot patterns and similarities, to make generalisations and to spot connections between different aspects of mathematics. The open-ended nature of this key strategy enables all children to contribute, regardless of their ability, and support can easily be added.

Tips for use

Introduce the two (or more) things that you want children to compare and simply ask: *What's the same, what's different?* This can work well individually, or through paired or grouped discussion. You could ask children to write their ideas on sticky notes and share these as a class, discussing each statement.

The strategy can be used with two things, but can also be effective when used with more as this can help develop children's ability to spot relationships. The strategy can also be used effectively alongside the 'Odd one out' strategy.

Key prompt questions can be provided to groups who may need more support, or more generally when you need to scaffold children's thinking in a particular direction. These could be provided in 'panic envelopes' (see the 'Problem-solving techniques' section for more details), which children should use only if they cannot think of anything that is the same/different themselves.

Watch out

Children may point out 'superficial' similarities/ differences (e.g. they are both numbers).

These should not be discouraged. The more often children are exposed to this strategy, the more 'mathematical' their responses will become. Providing prompt questions or panic envelopes can help children focus their thinking and produce deeper similarities/differences which demonstrate a greater level of reasoning.

Try these

Here are some examples to introduce your class to this strategy. In these examples, the content level is sometimes lower than that set out in the National Curriculum for Year 4. This is to allow children to focus on the development of reasoning skills, without being restricted by subject knowledge.

What's the same and what's different about 5555 and 5?
➤ Same: both are odd numbers; both are multiples of 5/in the multiplication table for 5
➤ Different: 5 is a 1-digit number, 5555 is a 4-digit number; 5 is the first multiple of 5

Case studies from the classroom

A snippet from a conversation between two Year 4 children discussing this question: *What's the same and what's different about a cube and a cuboid?*

What's the same and what's different about 19 and 21?
➤ Same: both are odd numbers; both are above 18; both are 2-digit numbers
➤ Different: 19 only has two factors (one factor pair), 21 has four factors (two factor pairs)

What's the same and what's different about multiplication and division?
➤ Same: they are inverse operations; both are operations
➤ Different: multiplication is commutative, division is not

What's the same and what's different about $\frac{3}{8}$ and $\frac{9}{24}$?
➤ Same: both are fractions; both denominators are multiples of 8; both are equivalent to $\frac{3}{8}$
➤ Different: denominators are different; $\frac{9}{24}$ can be simplified, $\frac{3}{8}$ cannot be simplified

What's the same and what's different about

 and ?

➤ Same: both are 2-D shapes; both are irregular quadrilaterals; both contain acute angles
➤ Different: one has two obtuse angles, one has only one obtuse angle

What's the same and what's different about

 and ?

➤ Same: both are times; both times are the same
➤ Different: one is on a digital clock, showing 24-hour time, the other is on an analogue clock

What's the same and what's difference about g and kg?
➤ Same: both are ways of measuring mass
➤ Different: they are different sizes: g is smaller than kg

Activities and investigations

1 The Queen's lawn mower
2 Patterns on digital clocks
4 Making 28
6 Crayon boxes
7 Delivery drones
8 Money mix-up
10 Flower symmetry
17 Revenge of the creepers

Child A: They both have 8 corners, and 12 vertices.

Child B: I think vertices are corners! They have 8 vertices and 12 sides.

Child A: Yes, you're right! They also both have 6 faces.

💡 Key strategy

Use the following question structures and routines alongside the other key strategies outlined in this book to help embed problem solving and reasoning into day-to-day mathematics teaching.

Zooming in

Give me a number, any number.
➤ *Zoom in so the number is greater than 2 000.*
➤ *Zoom in so the number is even.*
➤ *Zoom in so the number is a multiple of 10.*
➤ *Zoom in so the number is a multiple of 100.*
➤ *Zoom in so the number is <2 200.*

Draw me a 2-D shape, any 2-D shape.
➤ *Zoom in so it has straight sides.*
➤ *Zoom in so it is a quadrilateral.*
➤ *Zoom in so that it is an irregular quadrilateral.*
➤ *Zoom in so that it has one obtuse angle.*

What is the quickest or easiest way to … ?

➤ *count in nines from 0*
➤ *add four 2-digit numbers together*
➤ *quarter a number*
➤ *find $\frac{2}{3}$ of a number*
➤ *divide a number by 10*

What is/are … an example of?

➤ 9, 18, 27, 36 (numbers we say when counting in nines; multiples of 9)
➤ $\frac{4}{10}$, $\frac{6}{15}$ (fractions that show $\frac{2}{5}$)
➤ *4 000, 12 000, 8 000* (multiples of 1 000; multiples of 10; all even numbers; all multiples of 4)

How can we be sure that … ?

➤ *7 000 – 3 000 = 4 000*
➤ *all multiples of 6 are even numbers*
➤ *1 024 – 12 = 1 012*
➤ $\frac{3}{27}$ *is equal to* $\frac{1}{9}$

Is … a good example of … ?

➤ *a number that ends in 4 or 8 … a multiple of 4*
➤ *adding 0 to the end of a number … multiplying by 10*
➤ *taking 0 off the end of a number … dividing by 10*

🔍 Activities and investigations

3 The curious postman
5 A day in the life of a parking space
14 Mr Shah's swimming pool shambles
16 The search continues for the perfect planet!
17 Revenge of the creepers

Activities and investigations

1 The Queen's lawn mower

Learning objective
- To compare and classify geometric shapes, including quadrilaterals and triangles, based on their properties and sizes.

Reasoning skills
- Working systematically
- Finding all possibilities
- Making comparisons

Curriculum link
Geometry – properties of shapes

The problem

The Queen's lawn mower

Every morning, the Queen wakes up, looks out of her royal square window and admires the royal square lawn in the garden below.

She has recently employed a new royal lawn mower to keep the grass neat and tidy. He has come up with an idea to make the lawn a little more interesting.

The lawn mower decides to mow only lines that cut the whole lawn in half. He starts by mowing a diagonal line and it splits the square into two triangles.

The Queen is impressed. Are there any other shapes the lawn mower could make by mowing only one line across the square?

Things to think about:

- How many different ways are there to cut a square in half? (These are the different routes across the lawn the lawn mower can take.)
- How can you be sure that you have found all the different possibilities?
- As well as trying to give each shape a name, think about what its properties are.

Your challenge

Investigate the different shapes the Queen's lawn mower can make by mowing one, two, three or four lines across the royal lawn.

Background knowledge

- Children investigate the different shapes made when lines are drawn, bisecting a square.
- Children consider the different ways of drawing lines across a square so that it is split in half (there are four possibilities: a horizontal line halfway down, a vertical line halfway across and two diagonal lines). These are the only lines children can draw. They then consider different combinations of these lines and the shapes that are created as a result.
- Although the only lines children draw are those that would bisect a square, it is important that they do not think that the shapes created show halves, quarters and so on. Some combinations of lines will, others will not (see diagrams).
- As well as considering the different shapes and their properties, children could also consider the different fractions shown each time.

One line

Rectangles   Triangles

Two lines

Squares   Triangles and quadrilaterals   Triangles

Three lines

Triangles and squares   Triangles

Four lines

Triangles

Launching the activity

1. Prepare several examples of regular shapes cut out of paper. Ask children how the shapes could be folded in different ways so that each fold cuts the shape in half. For example, an equilateral triangle might be folded in three ways:

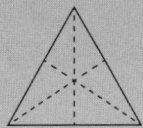

2. Display the prompt poster and discuss the scenario. Ask children how many different ways a square can be cut in half; ensure they understand that these are the only routes the lawn mower can take across the royal lawn. There are four:

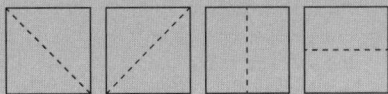

3. Discuss the different shapes made by one cut across the lawn. Ask children whether both sets of triangles/rectangles are the same. Can they prove this?

4. Ask children how they could make sure they have found all the possible shapes. Discuss different ways of recording their results. They may find Resource sheet 1.1 useful.

5. Give children time to explore the possible shapes by mowing one, two, three, then four lines across the lawn (see 'Background knowledge').

6. Encourage children to consider the properties of the shapes they create. *What do you notice about every single shape you make?* (They all have right angles.) Ask children to identify where they make shapes that are all equal in size. Use a graffiti maths approach where possible to help children record their findings.

7. Gather children together. Ask them to identify the shapes created and their properties.

8. As an extension, encourage children to consider the different fractions they have created. *Can we say what every shape is as a fraction? How?*

9. Finally, comment on the suitability of four cuts to create a Union Jack lawn design for the Queen!

Developing reasoning

➤ *Give me an example* of a way to split the square using two lines. What shapes do you make?
➤ *What do you notice* about every single shape you make?
➤ Do the lines **always, sometimes** or **never** split the square into equal shapes?
➤ Can you find a way to make two different sizes of triangles? **What's the same, what's different** about them?

Providing differentiation

Support
Give children squares of paper to fold three times. After folding, ask them to cut along each fold to compare the different shapes they have made. They could sort the shapes into sorting circles. Being able to rotate and flip shapes will allow children to see their similarities much more clearly. Children can then progress to the main activity.

Extension
Ask children to consider the shapes that can be made on a pentagonal (regular) royal lawn with different cuts. They can use Resource sheet 1.2 to record their findings.

Key strategies

1 Always, sometimes, never
5 Give me an example
12 What do you notice?
15 What's the same, what's different?

Problem-solving approaches

Graffiti maths

Taking it further

Use the idea of looking down on a shape to consider symmetry and lines of symmetry in different 2-D designs. For example, ask children to design a square flower bed for the Queen so that it has *x* lines of symmetry when she looks down on it.

Learning objective
- To solve problems involving 24-hour clock times.

Reasoning skills
- Convincing
- Working systematically
- Finding all possibilities
- Using numerical reasoning

Curriculum links
- Measurement – time
- Number – number and place value

The problem

Problem 2

Patterns on digital clocks

Jack looks at his digital clock next to his bed.
It reads: 11:11:11

He knows that, using the 24-hour clock, the time is 11 minutes and 11 seconds past 11 a.m.

Jack thinks, "I wonder how many times the digit 1 appears on a digital clock over a 24-hour period?"

Things to think about:
- Think about how often the numbers change in the seconds, minutes and hours.
- What patterns do you see? Are they always repeated?
- Make sure you are systematic in your recording – you don't want to miss one!

08:56:12   02:01:45   17:34:27

Your challenge

Identify how many times the digit 1 appears in the time on a digital clock, using hours, minutes and seconds, over 24 hours.

Year 4   More Problem Solving and Reasoning

Background knowledge

- Children investigate how many times the number 1 appears on a digital clock in 24 hours, using the 24-hour clock format and hours, minutes and seconds.
- Children will need prior experience of working with time and telling the time. They will need to know how digital clocks show the time and how time is displayed using the 24-hour clock.
- This activity will enable children to practise using the vocabulary of time, including the units and how they relate to each other: 1 minute = 60 seconds, 1 hour = 60 minutes, 1 day = 24 hours.

- It is important that children are encouraged to work systematically and make connections, e.g. working out how many times the 1 appears in the seconds digits within a minute and then multiplying this by 60 for each minute within an hour, then finding out how many times the 1 appears in the minutes digits within an hour and multiplying this by 24, and then finally focusing on how many times the 1 appears in the hours digits.

Launching the activity

1. Show children a time in hours, minutes and seconds using a digital clock, e.g. 19:20:24. *What does each number mean?* Encourage answers that use the correct vocabulary relating to hours, minutes, seconds and 'past'. *Is it in the morning or evening? Convince me that this is an evening time. What is the time using the 12-hour clock?* Re-cap the 24-hour clock.

2. Ask children what they know about measuring time. Again, encourage answers relating to hours and minutes and the relationship between the two: there are 60 minutes in an hour; the hour changes each time the minutes change from 59 to 60. Discuss how seconds relate to minutes. *What's the same, what's different about how minutes relate to hours?*

3. Show the prompt poster. 'Think, pair, share' about how to solve the problem. Ask children to convince their partner their strategy is the most efficient. Encourage them to be systematic and find all possibilities. *What would be a good time to start with? Does it matter what time you start with?*

4. Allow children time to start the task, using their chosen strategy. Encourage them to refine their strategy as they make connections and generalisations.

5. Use mini-plenaries to review progress and allow children to share any connections and generalisations. *What do you notice about your results so far? Can you see any patterns? What's the link between each hour within a 24-hour period?*

6. As a class, discuss the solution and the methods used. Emphasise that finding the final answer is less important than finding ways of working systematically and finding patterns. Ask some children to explain how they worked out the answer, focusing on connections and generalisations.

Developing reasoning

➤ *If the digit 1 appears 16 times in the seconds, in each minute,* **what else do we know**?
➤ **What do you notice** *about the results for seconds and the results for minutes?*
➤ **What's the same, what's different** *about the results for hours and minutes/minutes and seconds?*
➤ **What's the link between** *the patterns found in each hour within a 24-hour period?*

Providing differentiation

Support
Initially restrict the problem to finding out how many times the digit 1 appears between 10:00:00 and 11:00:00. Then extend the problem, encouraging children to make connections between the number of 1s that appear within the seconds and minutes times in each hour.

Extension
Children explore what other patterns they can spot on digital clocks over a 24-hour period. Ask children to work in pairs to create a different problem for another pair to solve, e.g. how many times are there only two different digits on the display (e.g. 12:12:12) or how many times are there where one digit is repeated five times (e.g. 14:44:44)?

Key strategies

12 What do you notice?
13 What else do we know?
14 What's the link between?
15 What's the same, what's different?

Problem-solving approaches

Think, pair, share; group work

Taking it further

Ask children to investigate whether they would get the same answer if they were using the 12-hour clock over a 24-hour period and explore which elements of their working and solution to this problem would stay the same and which would be different.

Learning objective
- To recall multiplication and division facts for multiplication tables up to 12 × 12.

Reasoning skills
- Conjecturing and convincing
- Working systematically
- Finding all possibilities
- Spotting patterns and relationships
- Using numerical reasoning

Curriculum link

1̲2̲3̲ Number – addition and subtraction; multiplication and division

The problem

Problem 3

The curious postman

Bob is a postman. He's really curious about numbers.

As he looks at each house number, he tries to discover patterns and interesting facts about them.

One day, he looks at house number 18.
He thinks to himself, "That's curious!"

18 **24** **12**

Things to think about:

- What does it mean to find the 'digit sum'?
- Can you think of a number where the digit sum is 6?
- Is the digit sum always a factor of the number itself? Can you spot any patterns?

"1 + 8 makes 9", he says. "And 9 fits into 18 twice.
That means that the number 18 is twice its digit sum:
$2 \times (1 + 8) = 18$."

Your challenge

Explore different 2-digit numbers that Bob might also be interested in.
Look for numbers that are twice (or three times, four times and so on) their digit sum.
How many can you find?

Year 4 — *More Problem Solving and Reasoning*

Background knowledge

- Children investigate the links between the digit sum and the number itself. They identify whether a 2-digit number can be found by multiplying its digit sum by another whole number.
- The digit sum is the total found by adding the number's digits together, e.g. the digit sum of 35 is 8 because $3 + 5 = 8$.
- Some numbers can be made by multiplying the digit sum by another whole number. For example, the digit sum of 12 is 3 ($1 + 2 = 3$) and four times this amount makes the number itself ($4 \times (1 + 2) = 12$); the number 12 is four times its digit sum.

- The 2-digit numbers that have a link between the digit sum and the number itself are 10, 18, 20, 21, 24, 27, 30, 36, 40, 42, 45, 48, 50, 54, 60, 63, 70, 72, 80, 81, 84 and 90. Children may be able to reason numerically why some of these numbers feature. For example, the multiples of 9 always have a digit sum of 9, so any of the multiples can be found by multiplying 9 by a whole number. The multiples of 10 are the result of multiplying a digit by 10; that digit is always in the tens place next to a 0 (so the sum will be equal to the digit itself).

Launching the activity

1. Show children the numbers 33, 15, 60 and 51. *What do you notice about the numbers? What's the same, what's different?* Take suggestions. If no one has mentioned it, highlight that the sum of each number's digits (the digit sum) is the same. Demonstrate how each pair of digits adds to 6 (3 + 3 = 6; 1 + 5 = 6; 6 + 0 = 6; 5 + 1 = 6).

2. Display the prompt poster and discuss it together. In pairs, ask children to explain, in their own words, the interesting fact that Bob notices.

3. Ask children to suggest numbers where the digit sum is 3. Collect several suggestions and then discuss whether any of them will divide by 3. *Give me an example of a number that can be divided by its digit sum.*

4. Discuss how the problem might be approached, e.g. starting from 10 and working upwards, or choosing numbers in any order and trying to spot patterns.

5. Allow children time to work on the problem in pairs. As they look for suitable numbers, observe the different strategies being used and whether children notice anything about the possibilities.

6. As a class, share their results. Ask how they found each possibility. Did they choose numbers randomly and see if they fitted the rule, or did they spot any patterns?

7. Write children's suggested numbers on the board (see 'Background knowledge' for all the possibilities). Ask what they notice about the answers and encourage them to give numerical reasons why certain numbers feature (and also why certain numbers do not).

8. As a plenary, ask children whether there are numbers where the difference between their digits fits into the number itself. *Why is this more difficult?*

Developing reasoning

➤ ***Give me an example*** *of a number that can be divided by the sum of its digits.*
➤ *42, 44, 48, 50: which is the **odd one out**? Why?*
➤ *Is it **always, sometimes** or **never** true that, when you add a number's digits together, the resulting number will divide into the original number?*
➤ *If the sum of its digits is 4, what is the number? If the sum of its digits is 4 and it divides by 4, what is the number?*
➤ *Is the activity **a good example of** finding whether the digit sum makes a factor of the number?*

Providing differentiation

Support
Encourage children to work through the 2-digit numbers from 10 systematically, as the lower numbers are easier to work with. Ask children to make each number with digit cards, then place them into a scaffolded sentence: __ + __ = __ (e.g. the digits in 12 could make 1 + 2 = 3). Children then arrange manipulatives in groups equal to the total of the digits (in this case, groups of 3) and try to make their original 2-digit number.

Extension
Encourage children to consider whether there are any 3-digit numbers that meet this rule. Consider how adding an extra digit (the 1 in the hundreds place) might affect any answers they found when thinking about 2-digit numbers.

Key strategies
1 Always, sometimes, never
5 Give me an example
7 If this is the answer, what's the question?
9 Odd one out
16 Other key questions

Problem-solving approaches
Pairs

Taking it further

There are many patterns involving digits of multiples of numbers and digit sums. Use the opportunity to investigate these further. For example, the sum of the digits of multiples of 3 always makes 3, 6 or 9. Encourage children to consider what happens when a total is a 2-digit number itself (they find the digital root by adding the digits together until they have a 1-digit answer).

4 Making 28

Learning objective
- To solve addition and subtraction two-step problems in contexts, deciding which operations and methods to use and why.

Reasoning skills
- Finding all possibilities
- Spotting patterns and relationships
- Making comparisons
- Using numerical reasoning

Curriculum link
Number – addition and subtraction

The problem

Making 28

Leah's favourite number is 28. She lives at number 28 and was born on 28 July.
She takes two dice and tries to make 28 with them. She can't roll a 28, but she does notice something interesting when she looks at the number on the top and the number on the bottom of each dice.

What does she notice?

Leah then has an idea. She puts her two dice together so that they are touching, face to face. She adds up all of the faces she can see and tries to arrange the dice so that the total equals 28.

Things to think about:
- Are dice numbered in a particular way?
- How many faces do two dice have?
- How many faces are hidden when you place them in the same way Leah does?
- How will you record your answers?

Your challenge

Find as many ways as possible of arranging the dice in a line so that the total of the faces you can see is 28.
For each arrangement that works, look at the two inner touching faces. What do you notice?

More Problem Solving and Reasoning

Background knowledge

- Children arrange two dice on a flat surface, end-to-end, so that the total of the visible faces is 28.
- A cube (and therefore a dice) has six square faces. By placing two dice end-to-end, four of the twelve possible faces are no longer visible (two on the base and two facing each other where the dice are touching). Children must arrange the dice so that the eight visible faces show numbers that total 28.

- Six-sided dice are numbered so their opposite faces add to 7 (when 1 is on the top, 6 is on the bottom, and so on).
- For every example of 28 they find, children should record the dice position and look at the two hidden faces that are touching each other; these should always equal 7. 14 + 7 + 7 = 28 so, when the two touching faces equal 7, the visible faces will always make 28.

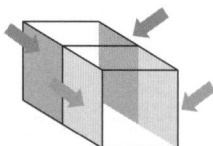

Each pair of opposite faces totals 7. These faces will always make 14, no matter how the dice are arranged.

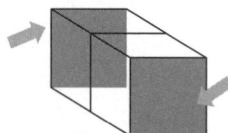

Where the middle hidden faces make 7, it means that their opposite faces on each end total 7 too.

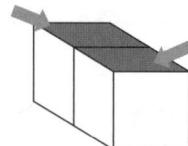

Finally, the way dice are numbered, the two top faces will equal 7.

Launching the activity

1. Show children a cube and discuss its properties. Ask how many faces it has. Ask how many faces they can see. Place the cube on a table and ask again.

2. Provide pairs or trios with two dice and ask them to find the total of the faces of one dice (6 + 5 + 4 + 3 + 2 + 1 = 21). Place a dice on a table and ask children what the highest visible total might be (20 if the face with the 1 is face down on the table). Ask children whether they can show the total 17 (by placing the 4 face down because 21 − 4 = 17).

3. Encourage children to look closely at each dice's numbering. Ask whether they think the dice are numbered a certain way. *What do you notice?*

4. Display the prompt poster and discuss the scenario. Ensure children understand the task and then discuss how they might record their answers. Give children time to explore different possibilities. For each example totalling 28, encourage them to record its make-up as well as what the two hidden faces are.

5. Bring children together and share results. Ask whether they have noticed anything about ways to make 28. *What's the same, what's different about the way you arranged your dice?* Can they spot any patterns?

6. Display two blank dice and discuss what else children know for different layouts. For example, what do they know about the four faces on the sides of the dice? *Is it always, sometimes or never true that they total 14?*

7. As a plenary, ask children to predict different hidden faces of dice, using their knowledge of the numbering pattern to help.

Developing reasoning

➤ *What do you notice* about the way that a dice is numbered?
➤ *Arrange* the dice in such a way so that the visible faces add up to 28.
➤ If one side of a dice shows __, *what else do we know?*
➤ *What's the same, what's different* about the way you have arranged your dice?
➤ Is it *always, sometimes* or *never* true that the total of the four faces on the sides of the dice is 14? Can you explain your answer?

Providing differentiation

Support
Ask children to place two faces of a dice together so that they equal 7 (e.g. a 3 and a 4). They should then find the total of the remaining eight visible faces. Provide number lines to help children keep track of the multiple-number addition.

Extension
Add an extra layer of challenge by asking children to complete the task without using dice. Instead provide them with images of nets of dice on Resource sheet 4.1. Children must visualise them without making them into cubes.

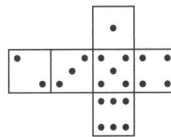

Key strategies

1 Always, sometimes, never
3 Arrange
12 What do you notice?
13 What else do we know?
15 What's the same, what's different?

Problem-solving approaches

Challenge trios; pairs; challenge setter

Taking it further

Ask children to explore different totals they can make using different numbers of dice placed end-to-end and placed so that some faces are obscured.

5 A day in the life of a parking space

<table>
<tr><td>

Learning objective
- To estimate, compare and calculate different measures, including money in pounds and pence.

</td><td>

Reasoning skills
- Working systematically
- Finding all possibilities
- Using numerical reasoning

</td><td>

Curriculum link

📊 Measurement – time and money

</td></tr>
</table>

The problem

A day in the life of a parking space

Su Sookey is a car park attendant. Her job is to ensure the smooth running of a multi-storey car park.

One day, Su thinks about how much money the car park is making. She watches one parking space and works out how much money it could earn in 12 hours.

HAMPTON STREET CAR PARK

Charges

Up to 1 hour	£1.75
Up to 3 hours	£4.75
Up to 4 hours	£6.50
Up to 6 hours	£10.00

Maximum stay 6 hours
OPEN 8 a.m. to 8 p.m.

Things to think about:
- How can the parking space make the most amount of money?
- How can the parking space make the least amount of money?
- Is there a way to work systematically to find all the possibilities?

For example, a car parking for 6 hours and 2 cars each parking for 3 hours would make £19.50 (£10 + £4.75 + £4.75).

Your challenge

What are the different amounts that one parking space could earn in a day?

Background knowledge

- In this activity, children investigate the total amount of money a parking space can 'earn' during a 12-hour day.
- The activity will help children to practise vocabulary associated with money (pounds, pence, total) as well as to practise the skill of adding money written in decimal form.
- Each parking ticket lasts for 1, 3, 4 or 6 hours. Therefore, children must find as many different combinations of 1, 3, 4 and 6 that equal 12 as possible (e.g. 6 + 6, 6 + 4 + 1 + 1 and so on). They must then find the cost of the parking tickets for each combination.

- Remind children that they are investigating the amount of money that is spent on tickets, rather than a particular sequence of numbers. So, if a car stays in the space for 3 hours, then another car for 6 hours and a final car stays there for 3 hours, this will yield the same amount of money as if the order was different (6, then 3, then 3, for example).
- For the purpose of the activity, presume that each car stays the full length of its ticket time.

Launching the activity

1. One of Philippe Dupasquier's *A Busy Day at the …* books would make an excellent introduction, encouraging children to think about events that happen over the course of a day in a particular place. Ask children what might happen during a day in the life of a parking space. *Who might use the space? How many cars might use it?*

2. Display the prompt poster. Read the challenge and look at the car park sign; point out the opening times. Ask children what the least number of cars might be over a 12-hour period (2 cars, each buying a 6-hour ticket). Encourage them to suggest how much money the parking space would 'earn' in this case (£20.00).

3. Ask children to suggest another way that the parking space could be used in a 12-hour period. Ask for another, another, another.

4. Discuss how children might record the different possibilities. Ask how they could work systematically to find all the solutions. Give children time to work in pairs to investigate the different possibilities.

5. In mini-plenaries, feed back strategies used to explore and record the problem, e.g. using pictures or diagrams to help. Ask whether they are using exchange strategies, e.g. children could exchange a 4-hour stay for one 1-hour stay and one 3-hour stay.

6. Bring children together to discuss their solutions and strategies used. Ask them to convince you that they have found all the possible totals. *If Su wants to make the most amount of money per space, what sort of tickets should she aim to sell?* Discuss how this is reflected in real life (100 cans of lemonade sold individually make more money than ten 10-packs of cans of lemonade).

Developing reasoning

➤ *Suggest a way that the parking space could be used during the 12 hours it is open.* **Another, another, another**.
➤ **Convince me** that you have found all the possible amounts the parking space can 'earn' in 12 hours.
➤ **What do you notice** about the different ways the parking space could be used?
➤ Is this investigation a **good example of** finding different ways to make 12?
➤ **What's the link between** pounds and pence?

Providing differentiation

Support
Encourage children to record the possibilities visually. For example, ask them to make towers of 12 cubes out of smaller towers of 1, 3, 4 and 6 cubes. How many different combinations can they use? Provide children with a simplified version of the problem (on Resource sheet 5.1) with the car park prices altered to £1.50, £4.50, £6.50 and £10.

Extension
Ask children to tackle this problem: *Su has decided to open the car park for 6 more hours. The new opening times are 6 a.m. to midnight. How much more money could each space make?*

Key strategies

2 Another, another, another
4 Convince me
12 What do you notice?
14 What's the link between?
16 Other key questions

Problem-solving approaches

Partner work

Taking it further

Ask children to consider other day-in-the-life-type problems. Give them a 24-hour day and ask how they could make it up using 12-, 8-, 6- or 2-hour blocks.

Learning objective
- To solve problems involving multiples.

Reasoning skills
- Convincing
- Working systematically
- Spotting patterns and relationships

Curriculum link
- Number – addition and subtraction; multiplication and division
- Measurement – money

The problem

Problem 6

Crayon boxes

Jordan needs to put 50 crayons into boxes.

He has some boxes that fit only 2 crayons, some that fit 3 crayons, some that fit 5 crayons and some that fit 6 crayons.

How can Jordan organise the crayons into different-sized boxes?

Things to think about:
- Can you group the crayons into equal groups to use just one size of box?
- What combinations of boxes can you use for 50 crayons?
- What apparatus could you use to help you?

Box of 2   Box of 3   Box of 5   Box of 6

Your challenge

Can you organise the 50 crayons in different boxes in lots of different ways?

Year 4   More Problem Solving and Reasoning

Background knowledge

- In this problem, children will explore ways to organise 50 crayons into different-sized boxes of 2, 3, 5 or 6.
- Children will need to use their knowledge of the four operations, especially multiplication and division, as well as multiples, to help them organise the crayons.
- Children will need to be systematic in their approach to ensure that they have thought about all the combinations of boxes which total 50 crayons. They should also see that they can exchange boxes to come up with a different solution, e.g. they could exchange one box of 5 for one box of 2 and one box of 3.

- There are many combinations to find. Whilst some children, who work systematically and make connections from the start, may find them all, the important thing is for children to show that they have thought about how to work systematically and made connections between the different sizes of groups. It is less important for children to find all combinations within the given time frame.

Launching the activity

1. Show children 10 crayons or pencils. Ask them to discuss, in trios, how they might organise these 10 crayons into three boxes, in different ways. Discuss possible solutions, e.g. all 10 crayons in one box, 5 in one box and 5 in another box (with the other box empty), 4 in one box and 3 in each of the other boxes, etc. Discuss how children might represent their findings.

2. Show the prompt poster. Ask children how they might organise the 50 crayons in different ways into boxes of 2, 3, 5 and 6. Ask children to give you some easy ways of sorting the crayons (e.g. 25 boxes of 2 or 10 boxes of 5). Ask for a harder way where a combination of multiples is used.

3. Children then continue working in their trios to find as many solutions as they can. Encourage them to work systematically and make connections. They should use graffiti maths, with large sheets of paper, to record and represent their working out and findings.

4. Use mini-plenaries to discuss strategies children are using. For instance, have they started with single or multiple solutions? How have they decided which multiples to combine? Have they been systematic in their approach? Have they thought about exchanging boxes from one solution to find a different solution?

5. Bring children back together and discuss the solutions and strategies they used. *What was the most obvious way to organise the crayons? Did anyone find a strange way to organise the crayons? Which of your solutions used the fewest boxes? Which of your solutions used the most boxes?*

Developing reasoning

➤ *Can you give me an **obvious** way to sort the crayons? Can you give me a **strange** way to sort them?*
➤ ***What's the same, what's different** between these two ways of sorting the crayons?*
➤ ***Convince me** you are working systematically.*

Providing differentiation

Support
Provide adult support to help children manipulate the practical resources, crayons or counters, boxes, number lines, etc. to sort them. Also, arrange children into mixed-ability trios to work through the problem.

Extension
Assign a price to each size of box and ask children to find combinations that will produce the greatest or smallest total cost.

Key strategies

4 Convince me
6 Hard and easy
10 Strange and obvious
15 What's the same, what's different?

Problem-solving approaches

Trios; graffiti maths

Taking it further

Look at different ways to organise things in the classroom or PE equipment to find out how to organise children or items into different groups of different sizes.

<table>
<tr>
<td>

Learning objective

• To describe positions on a 2-D grid as co-ordinates in the first quadrant and plot specified points and draw sides to complete a given polygon.

</td>
<td>

Reasoning skills

• Working systematically
• Spotting patterns and relationships
• Making comparisons
• Using numerical reasoning

</td>
<td>

Curriculum link

Geometry – position and direction

</td>
</tr>
</table>

The problem

Problem 7a

Delivery drones

A pizza delivery company is using drones to deliver pizzas.

It sends out four drones at a time and flies them in a square shape. Sometimes their signal cuts out!

The pizza company needs to work out where the missing delivery drones are before the pizzas get cold.

Here, one of the drone's signal has cut out. Can you tell where it is?

Things to think about:

• How are grids used to show the position of shapes and objects?
• Explain how you can remember how to use co-ordinates correctly.
• How much information do you need to know what the square looks like?

Your challenge

One day the signals of three of the drones cut out. The fourth drone is at point (5,5). What could the co-ordinates of the other drones be?
Look for patterns in the co-ordinates of each square you draw. What do you notice?

Year 4

More Problem Solving and Reasoning

Background knowledge

• Children investigate the co-ordinates of squares. They are asked to consider all the different squares possible when only one co-ordinate is given.
• Children will practise the language of position and direction, particularly terms such as up, down, left, right, and co-ordinates, as well as using co-ordinates correctly. In Year 4, children are expected to give co-ordinates in the first quadrant only, so only positive x and y values are needed.
• Children should initially focus on drawing squares where each side of a square is either a horizontal or vertical line of equal length

(they could later explore squares that are at an angle on the grid), so the co-ordinates of each corner are related. For example, a square may have corners (3,5), (3,9), (7,9) and (7,5).

• Children should notice the repeated numbers in the co-ordinates; this is because each corner is level with each other. They should also notice that the difference between some of the numbers is the same: 7 is 4 more than 3, 9 is 4 more than 5 (because each side of a square is the same length). Children could begin to generalise and see patterns in each set of co-ordinates.

Launching the activity

1. Ensure that children understand the role of each number in a set of co-ordinates. Display axes showing the first quadrant. Ask children to point to various co-ordinates. *How are grids used to show the position of things?*

2. Display the first prompt poster and discuss the scenario. Explain that children should only look at squares with horizontal and vertical lines. Look at the grid. In pairs, let children discuss how they know where the fourth drone is, then share their ideas.

3. Show the second prompt poster. Ask: *If the two points are two corners of a square, what else do we know?* Discuss how the square might be in either direction.

4. Show another set of two points on the third prompt poster; these are at opposite diagonal corners of a square. Ask children to complete the square.

5. Introduce the challenge. Provide children with Resource sheet 7.1 or a large grid for a graffiti maths approach. Encourage them to mark point (5,5) on their grids and then consider different squares that are possible using only horizontal and vertical lines.

6. Children should record the co-ordinates for each square that they find, look for patterns within them and generalise. *What do you notice about the co-ordinates of a square?*

7. Observe children working methodically, perhaps beginning with all possible 1 × 1 squares before moving on to 2 × 2 squares. Let them share their methods and say why they use this approach.

8. Ask children to share the different squares they found. List each set of four co-ordinates on the board. Let children consider the co-ordinates and identify any patterns. Encourage them to generalise: is there something they can say is always the case when plotting a square?

Developing reasoning

➤ (Show two points.) *If these are two corners of a square, **what else do we know?***
➤ ***Give me an example*** *of a square that has (5,5) as one of its corners.*
➤ ***What do you notice*** *about the co-ordinates of the points of a square?*
➤ ***What's the same, what's different*** *about the co-ordinates of a square?*

Providing differentiation

Support
Provide children with Resource sheet 7.2 and plastic counters. Ask children to place a counter on point (5,5) on the grid. They should use the different-sized squares on Resource sheet 7.3 to explore where they could put them to form different squares using counters.

Extension
Tell children that the drones are flying in a formation where the square is at an angle. Show examples of these on a grid, e.g.

Encourage them to look for patterns in the co-ordinates. *How are the patterns similar to the squares with horizontal and vertical sides?*

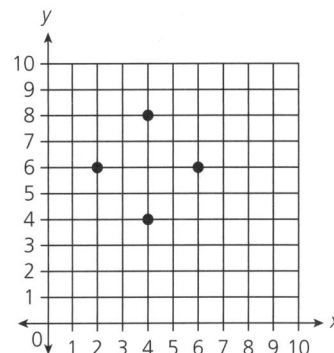

> ### Key strategies
> 5 Give me an example
> 12 What do you notice?
> 13 What else do we know?
> 15 What's the same, what's different?

> ### Problem-solving approaches
> Graffiti maths; large groups; pairs

Taking it further

Introduce the idea of translation of shapes and use the opportunity to encourage children to describe how squares have moved from one position to another within the first quadrant.

<table>
<tr><td>

Learning objective
- To solve addition problems involving money.

</td><td>

Reasoning skills
- Convincing
- Finding all possibilities
- Working systematically

</td><td>

Curriculum links

1,2,3 Number – number and place value; written calculations

Ill Measurement – money

</td></tr>
</table>

The problem

Money mix-up

Tamara buys a new scooter. It costs £19.95.
She pays using two notes and eight coins.

What is the least number of notes and coins she could have used to pay for the scooter?

What combination would have used the largest number of notes and coins?

Things to think about:

- Can you be systematic in your approach?
- Can you use column addition or multiplication to help you add up or multiply the money?
- Can you find all the possible combinations?

Your challenge

Explore all the possible ways you can make £19.95 using two notes and eight coins.

Background knowledge

- In this problem, children investigate all possible ways to pay for an item with a given number of notes and coins.
- Children will need to understand that, for this problem, the following notes and coins from the British monetary system could be used: £10 and £5 notes and £2, £1, 50p, 20p, 10p, 5p, 2p and 1p coins. Any value can be made from combinations of these notes and coins.

- Encourage children to write down all the possible combinations of monetary values so they can keep a track of the ones they have already used. Also encourage children to use exchanging methods to make different combinations, e.g. exchanging one £1 coin for two 50p coins.
- There are a number of solutions to this problem but, to work out all the possibilities, it is important for children to be systematic in their approach.

Launching the activity

1. Show children a £1 coin, two 20p coins, one 5p coin, two 2p coins and one 1p coin. Then show three 50p coins and finally show two 50p coins, two 20p coins and one 10p coin. *What's the same, what's different about these combinations?* Encourage children to notice that they are different coins but all are equal to £1.50.

2. Working with a partner, ask children to find three other ways of making £1.50 using only the coins outlined in Step 1. *Have you found all the possibilities? How do you know?* Challenge children to convince another pair that they have all the possibilities. Discuss how they know they have all the possibilities. If children have missed some out, ask them to explain why this might be, e.g. were they systematic in their approach? Share examples of possible combinations.

3. Show the prompt poster. Ask children to 'think, pair, share' how they might solve the problem and which strategies they might use. Discuss being systematic and using efficient methods, e.g. encourage children to work from a base of two notes (e.g. a £10 and £5 note) and then to work out the possible combinations from this base.

4. Set children off working on the problem in pairs. Use mini-plenaries to discuss how children are finding the solutions and what strategies they are using.

5. Bring children back together and go through the possibilities. Discuss what strategies they used and if they spotted any patterns in the solutions. Did they use exchanging methods, e.g. exchanging one £1 coin for two 50p coins or one 10p coin for two 5p coins? How can they be sure they found all the different possibilities?

Developing reasoning

➤ *If the answer is 95p, what's the question?*
➤ *Convince me you have all the possibilities.*
➤ Give me a **hard** example of making £19.95, and an **easy** example.

Providing differentiation

Support
Provide real or plastic money for children to manipulate the money needed and add the amounts together. Decrease the amount they need to find, e.g. £12.95, and concentrate on using smaller coins rather than notes.

Extension
Add in limitations to the problem, e.g. you can only use one £2 coin or you must use two 50p coins, etc.

Key strategies

4 Convince me
6 Hard and easy
7 If this is the answer, what's the question?
15 What's the same, what's different?

Problem-solving approaches

Think, pair, share; partner work; group discussion

Taking it further

Explore different ways of paying for things in real-life situations, e.g. *How many different ways can we find of paying for our school dinner?*

Learning objective	Reasoning skills	Curriculum link
• To solve problems involving increasingly difficult fractions. • To calculate quantities and fractions to divide quantities.	• Convincing • Finding all possibilities • Spotting patterns and relationships • Making connections	**1 2 3** Number – fractions

The problem

It's a fraction of feet

Roy, the circus ringmaster, has got into a bit of a muddle! He can see 64 feet and wheels in the circus ring.

He knows that $\frac{1}{4}$ of the feet belong to horses and that $\frac{1}{8}$ of the feet belong to acrobats.

Who could the other feet belong to?

The circus has **at least one** of each of these:
• horses with 4 feet
• dogs with 4 feet
• acrobats with 2 feet
• clowns with 2 feet
• unicycles with 1 wheel
• clown's bikes with 2 wheels.

Things to think about:

• Can you work systematically to find all the different combinations of feet and wheels that total 64?
• Can you write all your combinations as fractions?
• Will you use 64 as the denominator or can you simplify the fractions?
• Can you use practical equipment to help you with your additions and your fractions?

Your challenge

What animals, people or wheels might be in the circus ring?
Can you write each amount as fractions of the total?

Background knowledge

- In this problem, children explore possible solutions for combinations of feet and wheels in a circus ring that will total 64. They then write these combinations as fractions of the whole amount.
- Children may struggle with the concept of fractions of amounts. Explain that fractions are the proportion of a number or of a whole amount. All the fractions in this problem can be written using 64 as the denominator to show what proportion of 64 each amount is, e.g. $\frac{16}{64}$. The fractions can also be expressed in their simplified form, e.g. $\frac{1}{4}$, $\frac{1}{8}$, $\frac{1}{16}$, $\frac{1}{32}$, or as non-unit fractions, e.g. $\frac{3}{16}$, $\frac{10}{32}$.

- Children need to work systematically to ensure they find all possible combinations that total 64. They may start with the maximum number of dogs and minimum numbers of everything else, then reduce the number of dogs and increase the number of acrobats and so on.
- Children may benefit from using practical apparatus, e.g. interlocking cubes, counters or bead strings to manipulate the different ways of totalling 64.

Launching the activity

1. Ask for some examples of fractions. Discuss what a fraction means and let children 'think, pair, share' their ideas. Encourage children to use the words 'denominator', 'numerator' and 'equal groups'. Agree a definition of a fraction.

2. Show the prompt poster. In pairs, give children two minutes to calculate how many feet belong to horses and to acrobats. (It may be necessary here to review how to find fractions of amounts; see 'Background knowledge'.) *So, how many feet or wheels are left to sort out?* (40)

3. Let children discuss how to solve the problem, then share their ideas. Emphasise that the number of feet or wheels needs to be divided by the number of feet or wheels that each item has, to find the number of each item. For example, if 16 feet belong to dogs, there must be 4 dogs because dogs have 4 feet ($16 \div 4 = 4$).

4. Children should then work systematically to find different combinations, e.g. 4 horses (16 feet), 4 dogs (16 feet), 8 clown's bikes (16 wheels), 4 acrobats (8 feet), 2 clowns (4 feet), 4 unicycles (4 wheels): $16 + 16 + 16 + 8 + 4 + 4 = 64$.

5. Use mini-plenaries to feed back to the class. Encourage children to write each combination as fractions of the whole number: $\frac{1}{4}$ are horses, $\frac{1}{4}$ are dogs, $\frac{1}{4}$ are clown's bike wheels, $\frac{1}{8}$ are acrobats, $\frac{1}{16}$ are clown's feet, $\frac{1}{16}$ are unicycles. Fractions recorded in an unsimplified form are acceptable, e.g. $\frac{16}{64}$ clown's bike wheels. Encourage children to add the number of 64ths that they have in order to check that their total is 1 whole.

6. Share possible solutions and discuss efficient strategies to help solve the activity.

Developing reasoning

➤ *Give me an example* of a combination of feet/wheels to total 64. *Another, another, another*.
➤ *Convince me* that you have found all the possible feet/wheel combinations.
➤ We know that the total number of feet and wheels is 64. *What else do we know?*

Providing differentiation

Support
Children may lose track of their addition part way through. Provide practical equipment such as interlocking cubes or counters. Give children 64 of each object so that the total they have to play with never changes. Then ask them to manipulate these to find different combinations of groups that total 64.

Support those who may need additional help with recording fractions.

Extension
Ask children to come up with their own combination questions using fractions. They could use the same context of a circus with animals and wheels but with different numbers or they could use a different context.

💡 Key strategies

2 Another, another, another
4 Convince me
5 Give me an example
13 What else do we know?

⚙ Problem-solving approaches

Think, pair, share; partner work; group discussion

Taking it further

Build a fraction wall using strips of paper and use these to find how fractions relate to each other.

The problem

Flower symmetry

Mr Rake is designing a maths garden for children to use.

One of the features of the garden will be symmetrical rows of flowers. He has 8 flowers to plant in a row: 4 blue flowers and 4 yellow flowers. The row will be symmetrical.

Things to think about:
- Do you know what it means for something to be symmetrical?
- How could you model the different rows possible? You might like to draw each different coloured flower or use letters to represent them.
- How could you work systematically to make sure you've thought of all the possibilities?

Your challenge

How many different symmetrical rows of flowers can you plant using 4 blue and 4 yellow flowers?

Year 4 · More Problem Solving and Reasoning · Problem 10

Background knowledge

- Children investigate symmetrical patterns made by placing objects in a row (initially eight objects, four of each colour, but then extending to nine and then ten objects).
- Symmetry is the property of a shape or pattern where one half is exactly the same as the other, as though reflected across a line.
- A line of symmetry is a central line dividing a shape or pattern into reflected halves. Explain that lines of symmetry can exist in many directions (vertical, diagonal, horizontal) but, in this problem, children only focus on vertical lines of symmetry.

- With the initial eight-flower problem, this is a vertical line between the fourth and fifth flowers. As the problem develops using different numbers of flowers, this vertical line of symmetry will change (odd numbers are interesting as the line of symmetry will need to go halfway through the middle flower).
- Encourage children to work systematically, e.g. making all possible designs beginning with a particular sequence of colours.
- Children may notice that the challenge can be distilled to making different rows using four flowers (two of each colour) and then reflecting this to make a symmetrical eight-flower row.
- Use mirrors as a support.

Launching the activity

1. Before starting, prepare resources for children to explore and record answers (coloured cubes or counters, coloured pencils and small mirrors.

2. Display the prompt poster and discuss the arrangement of flowers. *What do you notice?*

3. Revise symmetry. Ask children for examples of symmetrical shapes and objects, particularly in the natural world.

4. Discuss the arrangement of flowers in the problem. *How can a row be symmetrical?* Initially, encourage children to use a vertical line of symmetry between the fourth and fifth flowers. Invite them to explore different ways of rearranging the flowers to find different solutions. Ask how they can do this systematically (e.g. by keeping the first colours the same and only changing the latter colours or by finding the opposite of a chosen string of colours by reversing them).

5. Allow children time to find as many solutions as they can. It is expected that this initial eight-flower problem should be used as a starting point before developing the problem further. Children should then investigate the number of possible symmetrical rows using nine (five blue, four yellow) and then ten flowers (five of each colour).

6. As a further development, take away the limitation of numbers of each colour. For example, ask how many symmetrical rows can be made using blue and yellow flowers (without specifying the number of each).

7. As a class, invite children to share their findings. Let them explain their working and how they knew all possibilities had been found. Look for evidence of systematic working, using a clear strategy. Encourage children to discuss the differences between finding solutions with nine and ten flowers.

Developing reasoning

➤ *What do you notice about the way these flowers have been planted?*
➤ *Organise these flowers so that they are symmetrical. **Another, another, another.** Can you do this systematically?*
➤ *If you were asked to rearrange four cubes (two of each colour) in as many different ways as possible, how would this compare to the eight-flower problem you were asked? **What's the same, what's different?***

Providing differentiation

Support
Provide children who struggle with the concept of symmetry with a row of four cubes (two of each colour). Ask them to complete the row with another four cubes so that it becomes symmetrical.

Provide blue and yellow cubes or counters so children can model each possible row of flowers (and therefore can see if they have repeated any of their rows). They could photograph their rows to record what they have already done. Begin with a six-flower problem if it is helpful for children to start with fewer possibilities.

Extension
Provide further arranging problems, e.g. *You have six cubes in a line, three blue and three green. How many different arrangements can you make?* Then ask: *How is this problem the same as the flower problem? How is it different?* Children may see that it is essentially the same problem. Ask them to change the problem so that it includes symmetry.

Key strategies

2 Another, another, another
12 What do you notice?
15 What's the same, what's different?

Problem-solving approaches

Challenge setter

Taking it further

Encourage children to explore examples of symmetry in the natural world. *Why are natural objects often symmetrical?*

Learning objective	Reasoning skills	Curriculum link
• To solve addition and subtraction two-step problems in contexts, deciding which operations and methods to use and why.	• Working systematically • Solving problems • Finding all possibilities	**1,3** Number – addition and subtraction

The problem

The partial pyramid

Have you ever made a number pyramid like this?
It begins with a layer of numbers across the bottom.
The numbers in each new layer are made
by adding the pair of numbers below.

	41	
22		19

10	12	7

Here is the second layer of a number pyramid. The pyramid
was started by putting eight different numbers from 1 to 20 as
the bottom layer.

20	23	15	19	33	32	16

Things to think about:

• How is each layer of a number pyramid formed?
• Can you explain the problem in a different way? What is it asking you to do?
• How could you work systematically to find the bottom layer?
• How will you decide which numbers to use, and in which order, in your own puzzle?

Your challenge

Which eight numbers were used to start the pyramid?
Can you find more than one solution?
Can you then create your own pyramid puzzle?
How can you arrange five different numbers from 1 to 10 along the base to find the largest total?

Background knowledge

• Children explore combinations of numbers to 20 that make given totals. This is done in the context of a pyramid puzzle, where each new number in the next layer of a pyramid is made by adding the two numbers underneath.

• This particular investigation works backwards. Given the second row of the pyramid, children are encouraged to think about the different possibilities of numbers on the base of the pyramid.

• Children will be encouraged to use the vocabulary of addition during the activity (total, sum, combine).

• Many children will begin to approach the problem using trial and improvement. Encourage them to think through the problem systematically instead. One way to do this is to begin with the number 1 digit card. Children keep going along the row until they cannot make the next total and so the sequence ends. They can then try starting with the number 2 digit card and so on. They should begin to see connections between the numbers in the row when different start numbers are used.

Second row totals: 20   23   15   19   33
                     / \ / \ / \ / \ / \
First row cards: 1 19   4 11   8   ?

Launching the activity

1. Discuss the Egyptian pyramids. *What were they built from? Were they built from the bottom up or the top down?*

2. Display the first prompt poster. Discuss number pyramids generally and work through the example on the second prompt poster. Show how each new layer is made by finding the totals of pairs of numbers underneath.

3. Return to the first prompt poster and to the pyramid for investigation. Explain that children will explore the base numbers. Remind them of the rules for the bottom layer: there are eight numbers between 1 and 20; none are repeated.

4. Look at the first brick in the second layer (20). Ask children to suggest combinations of numbers that might be underneath it (17 + 3, 6 + 14, etc.). *Another, another, another. How can you work systematically to find the bottom layer?*

5. Let children explore combinations of numbers to make the totals in the second layer. Use graffiti maths and encourage children to record both their failed attempts and their successes, using Resource sheet 11.1 if preferred.

6. Ask children who think they have found all possible combinations (there are two) to convince you that there are no more to find. Did they spot any connections between the numbers?

   The solutions are:

8	12	11	4	15	18	14	2
9	11	12	3	16	17	15	1

7. Share results as a class and discuss the strategies used. Challenge children to use Resource sheet 11.2 to continue the pyramid up to the apex. *What is the final total?*

8. Finally, using Resource sheet 11.3, ask children to create their own pyramid, using five numbers from 1 to 10 as the bottom layer. *How can you arrange the numbers to create the largest number at the top?*

Developing reasoning

➤ *Give me a way to make 20 using numbers to 20.* **Another, another, another.**
➤ *The first two squares add to make 20.* **What else do we know?**
➤ **Convince me** *that you have found all the ways to make the bottom row of the pyramid.*

Providing differentiation

Support
Provide children with a set of number cards, the second row written out and a number track to aid addition. Model a systematic approach and work through each addition with them. Where children have the total and one of the numbers, remind them that to find the second number they can count on from the first number until they reach the total.

Extension
Encourage children to invent their own similar challenges, using the blank pyramid on Resource sheet 11.4. Ensure that they also find the possible answers.

Key strategies

2 Another, another, another
4 Convince me
13 What else do we know?

Problem-solving approaches

Graffiti maths; mixed-ability working

Taking it further

The number pyramid can be used for many different investigations. For example, give children the apex of a pyramid and ask them to work downwards without getting to 0.

Learning objective
- To solve number problems involving number sequences and to count backwards through 0 to include negative numbers.

Reasoning skills
- Working systematically
- Finding all possibilities
- Making connections
- Spotting patterns and relationships
- Using numerical reasoning

Curriculum link
1,2,3 Number – number and place value

The problem

Problem 12

Sequences of signs

Maurice Myner positions signs along motorways. Each sign has the same distance between it. Here, the distance in between is 50 miles.

| 50 miles | 100 miles | 150 miles |

One day, Maurice has a different five signs waiting for him.

| 200 metres | 800 metres | | | |

He can paint any number he wants on the three blank signs.

Things to think about:

- How could you represent the five motorway signs?
- Is there a way to approach this problem systematically?
- How might you record the different sequences of the five signs you think of?

Your challenge

Find different sequences of five signs that include 200 and 800 metres.
The 200 and the 800 can go anywhere in the sequence of five.
What are the distances in between the numbers in your sequences?

Year 4   *More Problem Solving and Reasoning*

Background knowledge

- Children explore different five-number sequences that have the numbers 200 and 800 in them (where the intervals between the five numbers are the same). Although the problem is set within the context of motorway signs, encourage children to consider negative numbers, even though they won't be seen on a motorway sign!
- This investigation lends itself to a systematic approach. The obvious starting point is a sequence beginning with 200 and then followed by 800. As this will be a +600 sequence, the five numbers will be:
  200   800   1 400   2 000   2 600   (+600)

- Encourage children to alter the position of the number 800:
  200   500   **800**   1 100   1 400   (+300)
  200   400   600   **800**   1 000   (+200)
- Some children may explore sequences where the number 200 is not the first number (this is particularly interesting as it often results in negative numbers):
  −400   **200   800**   1 400   2 000   (+600)
- Another approach is for children to explore sequences that decrease rather than increase, e.g.
  800   600   400   **200**   0   (−200)

Launching the activity

1. Discuss motorway signs. Talk about what the numbers on them usually show (the distances to towns and cities) and how the distances are measured to work out what to put on the signs.

2. Display the prompt poster and discuss the scenario. Highlight that these motorway signs show distances in metres. Ask children where the 200 and the 800 could go in the sequence of five signs (e.g. the first two numbers). Using the 200, 800 … example, encourage children to work out the other numbers. *What is the rule for the sequence?*

3. Ask children how they could represent the five motorway signs to help record their ideas. *How might they record their different sequences?*

4. Discuss what 'systematic' means. *Can you think of a way to approach the problem systematically?*

5. Let children investigate different increasing sequences that involve the numbers 200 and 800 in mixed-ability pairs. Remind them to record the different rules for each sequence.

6. After a set time, regroup the class and talk about their findings. How many different sequences did they find? Write their results in a table according to the sequence rule. There should be four +600 sequences, three +300 sequences, two +200 sequences and one +150 sequence. *What do you notice about this total of ten different sequences? What would you expect the total to be if there were six motorway signs?*

7. Invite children to give a strange and an obvious example of sequences including the numbers 200 and 800. *Why are they strange or obvious?*

8. Ask children if this investigation could be done with any two numbers.

Developing reasoning

➤ ***Arrange*** the numbers 200 and 800 into different number sequences. What is the rule for each sequence?
➤ ***What's the link between*** the numbers in this sequence: 200, 800, 1 400, 2 000, 2 600?
➤ Give me a ***strange and*** an ***obvious*** example of a sequence involving 200 and 800. Why have you chosen these?
➤ ***What do you notice*** about the number of possible sequences?

Providing differentiation

Support
Provide children with number lines to help work out each jump.

Take away the 'finding the rule' aspect of the investigation. Give them the rule and encourage them to find the sequence by placing the numbers in different positions.

Extension
Encourage children to begin to consider what happens when the sequence continues below 0 and/or is a decreasing sequence.

Key strategies

3 Arrange
10 Strange and obvious
12 What do you notice?
14 What's the link between?

Problem-solving approaches

Mixed-ability working

Taking it further

Arranging children's results in table form (see 'Launching the activity') allows the 4 + 3 + 2 + 1 = 10 pattern to be seen. The number 10 is a triangular number and this is an interesting way to develop the investigation. How many triangular numbers can children find? Can they use them to predict how many possible sequences there might be if the original problem had ten motorway signs?

<table>
<tr><td>

Learning objective
- To solve problems involving fractions and to calculate quantities.

</td><td>

Reasoning skills
- Solving problems
- Making connections
- Using numerical reasoning

</td><td>

Curriculum link

1/2·3 Number – fractions (including decimals)

</td></tr>
</table>

The problem

Mixed-up offers

Jamie went into a shop and tripped over, knocking all the price tags onto the floor.

The shop had a sale on and the price tags had two parts: the fraction and the original price.

Using the price tags, you can work out the sale price.

Here are the parts to some of the price tags Jamie knocked over:

$\frac{5}{8}$ of $\frac{1}{2}$ of $\frac{1}{4}$ of $\frac{3}{4}$ of

£56   £80   £176   £72

Jamie stood on two other price tags with his muddy feet.

$\frac{1}{}$ ▩ of   £ ▩

Your challenge

How many different price tags can you make using the first eight price tags shown?
Work out the sale prices for each price tag you make.
What numbers could be on the muddy price tags if the sale price is £24?

Things to think about:

- How can you work out the sale price for each price tag?
- What could be the most expensive price tag Jamie knocked over? What could be the cheapest?
- How many different ways can you think of to make the number 24? How can you write this as a fraction of an amount?

Background knowledge

- In this problem, children are asked to use different parts of price tags (a fraction and a full price) to explore all possible prices in a sale.
- This activity will help children practise the language of fractions, including numerator, denominator, half, quarter, three-quarters, eighths and five-eighths.
- Children will already have experience of finding fractions of a discrete set of objects and will need to use these skills when finding fractions of prices.
- To find a unit fraction of a price (that is, a fraction with 1 as the numerator), children first need to divide the price by the denominator. This splits it into equal parts. To find a non-unit fraction of a price (that is, a fraction with a number other than 1 as the numerator, e.g. $\frac{3}{4}$ or $\frac{5}{8}$), they also need to multiply by the numerator to find the correct fraction. So, to find $\frac{3}{4}$, they divide by 4 (to give $\frac{1}{4}$) and then multiply by 3 (to give $\frac{3}{4}$).
- Provide counting equipment such as base 10 apparatus or cubes to help children visualise and embed the process of finding fractions of amounts.

Launching the activity

1. Discuss how shops use fractions when there is a sale on (half-price sale, one-third off).

2. Ask children to suggest fractions. Write some on the board and ask children to identify what each part of a fraction tells them, using precise vocabulary.

3. Display the prompt poster. Ask children to suggest a price tag that they can make by combining a fraction and an amount from the first eight price tags. Ask for another, another, another. Ask how they could work to ensure they can find them all.

4. Revise finding fractions of amounts (particularly $\frac{3}{4}$ and $\frac{5}{8}$ as they are not unit fractions and therefore involve an extra step).

5. Let children work through the problem in pairs, finding all the possible amounts.

6. Regroup the class and ask what prices children recorded for the first part of the problem. *Can you see any links between any of the prices?* (E.g. they may spot that $\frac{1}{2}$ of a number is twice as big as $\frac{1}{4}$ of a number or that $\frac{1}{2}$ of a number plus $\frac{1}{4}$ of a number is the same as finding $\frac{3}{4}$ of a number.)

7. Let children explore the different ways of making £24 with the two 'muddy' price tags. In their pairs they should discuss their methods and why these work.

8. Refer back to the links between the prices in the first part of the problem (step 6). How did these links help them investigate the different combinations of price tags to make £24?

9. Ask children for facts about the number 24. *What are the multiples of 24?* Did they use multiples when making price tags with unit fractions (e.g. $\frac{1}{2}$ of 48)? *What are the factors of 24?* How did these help them to write price tags with non-unit fractions (e.g. $\frac{3}{8}$ of 64)?

Developing reasoning

➤ *Suggest a price tag that you can make.* **Another, another, another.**
➤ *Which are the cheapest and the most expensive prices you can make using the price tags?* **Convince me.**
➤ *If $\frac{1}{4}$ of a price is £75,* **what else do we know?**
➤ *Give me a* **hard and** *an* **easy** *'fraction of a price' problem.*
➤ *Give me some multiples and factors from the* **maths story** *of 24.*

Providing differentiation

Support
Give children the same problem, but with unit fractions only ($\frac{1}{2}$, $\frac{1}{4}$ and $\frac{1}{3}$) as well as 2-digit prices that will give whole numbers (£36, £60, £12). Provide children with counting equipment to help find fractions of these numbers.

Extension
Ask children to devise their own 'fraction of a price' problems for their peers to solve. Ask them to write a hard and an easy problem and ensure that they can work out the answer themselves before sharing it with peers.

Key strategies

2 Another, another, another
4 Convince me
6 Hard and easy
8 Maths stories
13 What else do we know?

Problem-solving approaches

Pairs; challenge setter

Taking it further

Use the opportunity to develop children's understanding of finding fractions of quantities. This might entail activities based on length (e.g. designing a football pitch $\frac{1}{4}$ of the size of a full-size pitch) or mass (e.g. altering a recipe for 12 by finding $\frac{1}{3}$ of the ingredients so that it feeds 4). Whatever the challenge, ensure all quantities are divisible by the denominator and give an integer as an answer at this stage.

Learning objective
- To find the area of rectilinear shapes by counting squares.

Reasoning skills
- Solving problems
- Making comparisons
- Using numerical reasoning

Curriculum link
Measurement – area

The problem

Problem 14

Mr Shah's swimming pool shambles

Mr Shah lays tiles for swimming pools.
He uses a machine to cut tiled flooring to fit any shaped swimming pool that has straight lines and right-angled corners.

Today he has a problem. His machine is cutting pieces of flooring to the correct shape, but halving the dimensions of the actual swimming pool! For example:

The flooring cutter cuts this:

for a pool with these dimensions:

The flooring cutter cuts this:

for a pool with these dimensions:

Your challenge

Mr Shah finds a way of using the pieces his machine cuts to fit the actual pool. What do you think he does?
Does this only work for squares and rectangles? Try some of these other shapes.

Things to think about:
- What is the area of a shape?
- If the length and the width of a shape are doubled, what happens to the area? Is this always true?
- What could you do to find out whether the smaller pieces will fit the larger swimming pool?

Year 4

More Problem Solving and Reasoning

Background knowledge

- Children use the context of swimming pool tiled flooring to investigate ways of making rectilinear shapes using smaller versions of the same shape, whose dimensions are half that of the original.
- Children use the vocabulary of shape names (square, rectangle) and measure (length, width, area).
- The area of a shape is the space within it. In Year 4, children are expected to understand this concept but not to work it out using a formula. Instead they are encouraged to find the area by counting squares.

- Children will find that they can make the flooring fit the pool shape by using four of the smaller pieces (i.e. four 1×1 squares will fit a 2×2 square, four 1×3 rectangles will fit a 2×6 rectangle and so on). This works for other rectilinear shapes, although shapes will have to be rotated and flipped to fit together.
- A common misconception is that, if a shape's dimensions are doubled, its area will also double. In fact, if a shape's length and width double, its area will quadruple. Shapes that triple their dimensions increase their area by nine times, shapes that quadruple their dimensions increase their area by 16 times and so on (these are all square numbers).

Launching the activity

1. Recap the meaning of area. In pairs, ask children to create a definition for area, giving an example if they can. Share definitions and agree on a class definition.

2. Remind children how to find the area of a rectilinear shape. Draw several examples on the board and ask children to count the squares. Ask them what they think will happen to the area of a shape if the dimensions of each side are doubled.

3. Display the prompt poster and discuss the scenario. Look at the examples of the square and rectangle. *What's the link between the area of a shape and the same shape with the dimensions doubled?*

4. Ask children whether they can see what Mr Shah can do with the pieces his machine is cutting. Give them time to explore whether the four-shape rule works for other squares and rectangles.

5. Split children into mixed-ability groups and give them further time to investigate other rectilinear shapes. Provide them with squared paper to explore reflecting, rotating and flipping shapes in order to see whether four of them will fit inside a shape whose side lengths are all doubled.

6. Encourage children to explore their own rectilinear shapes. *Is it always, sometimes or never true that four rectilinear shapes will fit inside the same shape, with double the dimensions?*

7. Gather the class together and share results. How did children manage to fit the shapes together? Did they use a strategy? Encourage them to answer using words like 'rotate' and 'flip' as well as positional words.

8. Ask children whether they have found any exceptions to the four-shape rule. Discuss why these do not work.

Developing reasoning

➤ Is 'the space inside a shape' **a good example of** 'the area of a shape'?
➤ **What's the link between** the area of a shape and an area of the same shape with double the dimensions?
➤ Draw a **hard** and an **easy** example of a shape that will fit four times inside a shape with double the dimensions.
➤ Is it **always, sometimes** or **never** true that four rectilinear shapes will fit together to make the same shape, but with double the dimensions?

Providing differentiation

Support
Encourage children to investigate different squares and rectangles. Provide them with Resource sheet 14.1 which has shapes to cut out, and use these shapes with centimetre-squared paper. Encourage children to put them together like a jigsaw before counting each square to find the area.

Extension
Ask children to explore the link between the way a shape increases and the change in its area. They already know that doubling the length and width results in a quadrupling of the area. What happens if the shape's dimensions become three/four/five times as big? The pattern will be one of square numbers (see 'Background knowledge').

Key strategies

1 Always, sometimes, never
6 Hard and easy
14 What's the link between?
16 Other key questions

Problem-solving approaches

Mixed-ability working

Taking it further

Give children a limited number of squares (e.g. six) and ask them to make as many rectilinear shapes as possible by putting the squares together (i.e. each shape has an area of six squares). How many shapes can they find?

Learning objective
- To multiply 2-digit and 3-digit numbers by a 1-digit number (using a formal written layout).

Reasoning skills
- Conjecturing and convincing
- Solving problems
- Making connections
- Using numerical reasoning
- Using algebraic reasoning (see 'Taking it further')

Curriculum link
Number – multiplication and division

The problem

Mission multiply

Problem 15

A series of alien calculations has been found.
Look carefully at them:

1. (alien symbols calculation)
2. (alien symbols calculation)
3. (alien symbols calculation)

Clues: (alien symbol clues)

Things to think about:
- How do you multiply a 3-digit number and a 1-digit number vertically?
- Can you make any statements about the numbers in the first multiplication?
- Can you see any parts of the multiplication that give a clue about what digits they are?

Your challenge

Think carefully about the digit that each symbol could represent.
Find as many different multiplications as you can that fit each calculation.
Some may have one, some may have several.
As you work through the multiplications, you may change your answers!

Year 4

More Problem Solving and Reasoning

Background knowledge

- Children explore different multiplications that could be represented by a set of symbols. They should use their knowledge of both multiplication table facts and vertical multiplication to find different multiplications that fit the given symbols.
- The formal written layout for multiplying a 3-digit number by a 1-digit number is where both numbers have been written vertically. The numbers are multiplied column by column from right to left. In this particular example, there are two addition clues to help children work out the missing digits in the calculation.

- Children should be encouraged to explore ideas initially and then begin to make numerical observations about the digits (e.g. the first multiplication shows the same digit multiplied by itself, resulting in a number that ends with that same digit again. The only square numbers that obey this rule are $5 \times 5 = 25$ and $6 \times 6 = 36$ so these are the two possible answers).
- If necessary, revise the formal written method at the start of the session, linking it to the array method.

Launching the activity

1. Explain that this challenge is all about symbols aliens might use instead of our digits! Ask children to suggest some types of symbols.

2. Briefly revise the formal written method of HTO × O.

3. Display the prompt poster and discuss the scenario. Ask children to suggest how to approach the problem. Allow time to try different digits and begin to notice characteristics about them.

4. Encourage children to consider the first two multiplications, looking at the symbols to work out facts about them (e.g. the first multiplication shows two of the same digit (a square number) and the answer ends with the same digit; the second multiplication shows two different digits and the answer ends with the same digit as the first multiplication). These two clues will help them come up with different suggestions.

5. Ask: *What else do we know about the digits in the third multiplication?* Children may find the two additions helpful in giving clues (e.g. in the second clue, the second digit must be 0: when it is added to a symbol, the symbol stays the same). Provide further time for exploring possible multiplications.

6. Allow children time to use numerical reasoning to deduce the value of each symbol. Encourage them to make links between all of the calculations on the prompt poster, using later information to adjust their previous guesses.

7. Regroup the class. Discuss their different multiplications and how they found them.

8. As a plenary, ask children to convince you that the symbols they have worked out are correct.

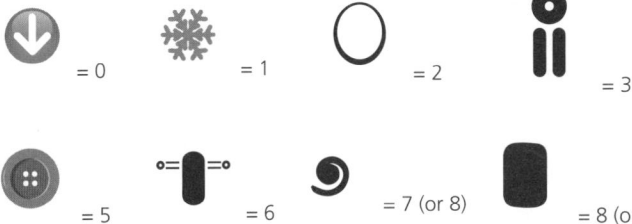

Developing reasoning

➤ *The first multiplication is a square number.* **What else do we know?**

➤ **Convince me** *that the digits you have chosen for each symbol are the correct ones.*

➤ *Can you write your own* **hard** *and* **easy** *symbol problems? What makes them more difficult or easier?*

Providing differentiation

Support
Practise multiplication table facts by giving children a fairly open-ended multiplication to investigate (e.g. give them the second multiplication, without the first to limit it). Children could fill in a multiplication square and use their answers to find numbers easily.

Extension
Ask children to develop their own multiplication symbol challenges, checking that they give just enough clues for others to be able to work out the answer.

Key strategies

4 Convince me
6 Hard and easy
13 What else do we know?

Problem-solving approaches

Mixed-ability working; challenge setter

Taking it further

Introduce the idea of aliens using one symbol to represent an entire number. This is a pre-algebra concept and children should be able to understand it.

Ask children to write their own number sentences using 'human' numbers and one 'alien' number, e.g. $9 \times \Diamond = 108$. Children work in pairs to decide how to find the alien numbers.

= 0   = 1   = 2   = 3

= 5   = 6   = 7 (or 8)   = 8 (or 7)

16 The search continues for the perfect planet

Learning objective
- To count in multiples of 6, 7, 9, 25 and 1000.

Reasoning skills
- Working systematically
- Spotting patterns and relationships
- Using numerical reasoning

Curriculum link
1/2/3 Number – multiplication and division

The problem

Problem 16

The search continues for the perfect planet!

The crew of a spaceship is hunting for the perfect planet. There are hundreds of possible planets for the spaceship to visit. They all have a different number, from 1 onwards.

There are nine features the astronauts need to consider:
1. Every second planet has clean air.
2. Every third planet has gravity similar to Earth.
3. Every fourth planet has an excellent landing spot.
4. Every fifth planet has water.
5. Every sixth planet has a natural food supply.
6. Every seventh planet has a climate like Earth's.
7. Every eighth planet has evidence of life.
8. Every ninth planet has its own natural resources.
9. Every tenth planet is just the right temperature.

115

108

40

30

18   24

Things to think about:
- What strategies can you use to count in twos, threes, fours, fives, sixes, sevens, eights, nines and tens? Are any of these related?
- How will you record your results?
- Do you think any planet number will have all nine features? What sort of number would you expect a perfect planet to be?

Your challenge

Which planets have **none** of the features the crew is looking for?
Will the spaceship crew have to settle for a planet with several of the features, but not all?
How close to a perfect planet can you get?

Year 4

More Problem Solving and Reasoning

Background knowledge

- In Year 3, this problem was explored as a spaceship crew searching for the perfect planet, counting in steps of 2, 3, 4, 5, 8 and 10 (beyond 100). In Year 4, we build on this by including steps of 6, 7 and 9 and by considering numbers that are multiples of as many of the numbers 2 to 10 as possible.
- Children count in multiples of 2, 3, 4, 5, 6, 7, 8, 9 and 10 to see which numbers occur in each count (in particular, which numbers are not counted at all and which numbers occur in several counts).
- The multiple of a number is a product of that number and another whole number. A factor is

a number that a larger number can be divided by without leaving a remainder. To solve this problem, children will search for numbers with the most factors.

- As it is necessary to keep counting past 10× each number, children may find a 100 square helpful to support counting in steps and recording results. Encourage them to place markers to show which numbers feature (e.g. yellow counters on every second number, red counters on every third number and so on). There will be patterns to spot with each of these multiples.

Launching the activity

1. Ask children what conditions they would look for to survive on a planet. Discuss whether it is essential to have all these conditions or just some.

2. Display the prompt poster and discuss the conditions. Begin with the need for a natural food supply and ask what 'every sixth planet' means. Discuss the equipment children could use to help count in sixes. Ask them to give a number they would say if they were counting in sixes. Ask for another, etc.

3. Ask children how they could record which numbers are in each sequence. Explain that they must find a planet that is as near to perfect as possible. Split children into pairs and give them time to find the multiples of 2, 3, 4, 5, 6, 7, 8, 9 and 10. They could use Resource sheet 16.1 to record their counts.

4. Ask pairs what they notice about the multiples of 2, 3, 4, 5, 6, 7, 8, 9 and 10 (in particular whether they think any are related). Provide access to panic envelopes containing 100 squares with the first 10 multiples of a number shaded and this question: *What do you notice about these multiples? Is there a quick way to find them?*

5. Regroup the class to share their findings. Ask children to identify the planets they would avoid (with no suitable conditions). *What do you notice about these numbers?* (All are odd numbers.) Can they explain why this is? Why will the planets that have an excellent landing spot and a natural food supply always also have clean air?

6. Children should work until they have gone through all the multiples of 2, 3, 4, 5, 6, 7, 8, 9 and 10. *Which are the nearly perfect planets? Why is it that these are often multiples of 3 that are even?*

7. Challenge children to identify the next nearly perfect planet. *Convince me why this is. Is there a way to test whether it is always true?*

8. Finally, discuss whether there is a way to know if a number is a multiple of 2, 3, 4, 5, 6, 7, 8, 9 or 10 without counting in twos, threes, etc. Encourage children to describe the patterns of multiples they noticed.

Developing reasoning

➤ *Give me a number you would say if you were counting in sixes. **Another, another, another.***
➤ ***What do you notice** about the planets you would want to avoid?*
➤ ***Convince me** of the next planet number to have six or more factors.*
➤ ***What is the quickest or easiest way to** find a number that is a multiple of 2, 3, 4, 5, 6, 7, 8, 9 and 10? Are any of these multiples related?*

Providing differentiation

Support
Initially limit the problem to counting in twos, threes, fours, fives and tens. Once children have mastered this, introduce further conditions.

Extension
Encourage children to consider the properties of the nearly perfect planets in more detail. Is there a pattern to them? Planets with six factors between 2 and 100 are 60, 72 and 90. What do children notice about these numbers? Ask them to write rules for a nearly perfect planet (e.g. must be even, must be a multiple of 3) and then to test their rules.

Key strategies

2 Another, another, another
4 Convince me
12 What do you notice?
16 Other key questions

Problem-solving approaches

Pairs; panic envelopes

Taking it further

Challenge children to find rules to identify which planets are in which sequences. For example, multiples of 10 always end in a 0; the digits in multiples of 9 always add to make 9.

Learning objective
- To solve problems involving multiplying and adding, including harder correspondence problems.

Reasoning skills
- Working systematically
- Solving problems
- Finding all possibilities
- Using numerical reasoning

Curriculum link
1.3 Number – multiplication and division

The problem

Problem 17

Revenge of the creepers

An intergalactic gardener has been asked to report back to Earth about what is growing in her space station greenhouse.

There are two types of plants growing there:
1. The Ziggle plant is a harmless creeper, good for providing shelter and its leaves taste delicious in a salad.
2. The Zorgon plant is a carnivorous creeper. Astronauts shouldn't get too close to it if they want to keep their fingers!

Unfortunately, both plants look the same. The only way to tell them apart is to count their leaves.
Ziggles have 3 leaves and Zorgons have 4.

Things to think about:
- What is the difference between the Ziggle and Zorgon plants?
- If the gardener counts 8 leaves, which plants are in the greenhouse? What about 12 leaves?
- Can you use exchange methods to find a different combination, e.g. 4 Ziggles have the same number of leaves as 3 Zorgons. Does this help?

Your challenge

The gardener counts 62 leaves altogether.
How many Ziggle and how many Zorgon plants could there be?

Year 4 — More Problem Solving and Reasoning

Background knowledge

- Children are presented with a greenhouse containing 62 leaves and two possible plants that might be growing there (one with 3 leaves, the other with 4). They investigate combinations of multiples of 3 and 4 that equal 62.
- A multiple of a number is the result of multiplying that number by another whole number. Children will practise multiples of 3 and 4 and explore combinations of those numbers.

- Some children may initially take a trial-and-improvement approach, choosing a multiple of 3 and seeing whether there is a multiple of 4 that will equal 62 when combined with it. Others may try drawing the plants or use counting equipment as a support.
- A systematic way to find all the possibilities is to start with one type of plant each time and gradually see whether it is possible. A table could be used to collate results and reveal patterns. A table may begin as follows:

No. of Ziggle plants	No. of Ziggle leaves	No. of leaves remaining	No. of Zorgon plants	Combinations
1	3	$62 - 3 = 59$	Not possible	
2	6	$62 - 6 = 56$	$56 \div 4 = 14$	2 Ziggles and 14 Zorgons
3	9	$62 - 9 = 53$	Not possible	